CR&O

This publication is designed to provide current information in regard to
the resources and services in Rhode Island available to both seniors and
disabled individuals, as well as their families, caregivers, and professionals involved in the care of seniors and disabled individuals. It is sold with
the understanding that the publisher and author is not engaged in
rendering legal or other professional services. If legal advice is required,
the services of Laura M. Krohn can be sought privately by calling
(401) 398-8383.

- Partially from a Declaration of Principles jointly adopted by a
Committee of the American Bar Association and a Committee of
Publishers and Associations.

ISBN No. 978-0-9815005-7-7

Printing of this edition of the Senior Resource Guide was made possible
by the nursing homes, home health care agencies, independent living
residences and assisted living residences listed herein.

Printed by Image Printing

33 Plan Way, Warwick, Rhode Island.

Welcome to the Special Fifth Edition of the Senior Resource Guide of Rhode Island, a comprehensive guide to services and resources in Rhode Island available to seniors, their families, caregivers, and advocates.

This compilation encompasses all resources available to advocate for the physical, emotional, legal, financial, and spiritual needs of seniors, their families, and caregivers.

With over sixty topics, including Senior Housing, Health Care Options, Alzheimer's Disease and Dementia, Geriatric Care Management, Medicaid for the Nursing Home, Hospice, Elder Abuse, Caregiver Support, Transportation, and many other professional and personal resource information, the Guide will serve as an essential tool to navigate through the overwhelming long-term care process.

TABLE OF CONTENTS

TABLE OF CONTENTS

TABLE OF CONTENTS

HOME HEALTH CARE OPTIONS

WHAT IS HOME HEALTH CARE?

Home care typically refers to medical and/or non-medical services that assist individuals with activities of daily living.

Home care is becoming an increasingly popular choice for care because it enables individuals to remain in their own environments longer and helps families better plan for the future care of a loved one.

Many families utilize home care agencies to supplement the services they cannot perform themselves for a loved one due to work and other family commitments. These agencies provide an extra pair of hands and assist in the overall care management of a loved one.

Most agencies can provide services for as little as six hours a week up to 24 hours a day, seven days a week. The schedules are usually determined during the assessment process and vary depending on the needs of both the family caregiver and the needs of the client.

Caregivers need to be reminded that they are at health risk if they try to take on too much and forget to take care of themselves. It is just as important that the caregiver is getting proper nutrition, rest, and exercise as it is for the person they are caring for.

The Facts About Home Care

- Falls are the leading cause of home injury.

- People aged 75 years and older who fall are four to fives times more likely to be admitted to a Long-Term care facility for a year or longer.

- Nearly 25% of American adults provide assistance to a parent or relative.

- One in four caregivers say the person they care for lives with them.

Difficulties Caregivers Experience:

- Burnout
- Stress
- Other family / job responsibilities
- Struggle to balance tasks
- Health problems

Who may need non-medical Home care?

- Seniors who are living at home and having difficulty performing their *IADLs*. (*Instrumental Activities of Daily Living*)

What are Instrumental Activities of Daily Living (IADLs)?

- Using the telephone
- Grocery Shopping
- Preparing Meals
- Managing Money
- Doing Laundry
- Opening Mail
- Getting to places beyond walking distance
- Taking Medications
- Doing Housework

What are Activities of Daily Living (ADLs)

- Bathing Assistance
- Dressing
- Feeding
- Transferring (non-ambulatory)
- Toileting
- Nail Clipping
- Brushing Hair
- Administering Medications

Medical vs. Non-Medical Home Care Agencies

Non-Medical agencies	Medical Agencies
Provides Caregiver assistance to those who are having difficulty performing their IDALs	Provides nursing care to those who cannot perform their ADLs
Provides Companionship and Homemaker services ensuring a safe setting	Personal care specialists who provide or assist with personal care, ambulating, incontinence management, and feeding
In-house safety assessments	In-house safety assessments
Prompting and cueing for Activities of Daily Living	Brushing hair, toileting, feeding, hands on assist in doing personal hygiene
Medication Reminders	Administer Medications
Stand-by assistance for bathing	Bathing – hands on
Meal preparation, light housekeeping, laundry, transportation, companionship, sitting services	Will usually refer out to a non-medical home care agency that provides housekeeping, companionship, and sitting services

What Are Some Important Questions To Ask When Making A Decision On An Agency?

Non-Medical Agencies	Medical Agencies
What services are performed?	What services are performed?
Are the caregivers bonded and insured?	Are the certified nursing assistants bonded and insured?
Are your caregivers trained and supervised?	Does your staff work under the supervision of a Registered Nurse?
What are your backup procedures for a no show?	What are your backup procedures for a no show?
How is communication with the family maintained?	How is communication with the family maintained?
Do you have a 24-hour on call supervisor?	Do you have a 24-hour on call supervisor?

Funding For Medical vs. Non-Medical Home Care

Non-Medical Home Care	Medical Home Care
Private Pay	Private Pay
Long Term Care Insurance	Most Insurance's including long term care insurance
State funding if eligible	Medicare/Medicaid

—What to Ask—

The following are some questions you should ask when choosing a home care agency:

- **Is the agency licensed by the R. I. Department of Health?**

    State licensed agencies are required to meet rigorous quality standards such as background checks, educational requirements and employee health screenings. For this reason, only licensed agencies are certified to provide hands-on care for your loved one. While many companies may *propose* that they follow strict guidelines, licensed agencies must *comply*, and they are routinely surveyed for compliance.

- **Does the agency offer health services or strictly companion care?**

    Sometime you can use two different agencies, depending on your needs.

- **Is there a high turnover of employees within the agency?**

    It is difficult for a senior or disabled individual when home care involves meeting new caregivers on a regular basis. Most seniors and disabled individuals favor routine and consistency.

- **How long has the Agency been in business?**

    This isn't always dispositive, but as a rule, with longevity comes stability and expertise.

- **When you call the agency, how are you received?**

    Can you talk with a live person, or are you requested to leave a call back number? Is the person handling your call concerned and knowledgeable? Responsiveness is very important when you are dealing with issues involving health and family. This is particularly true if the family is not local and relies heavily on the agency to provide care to their loved one.

DIVISION OF ELDERLY AFFAIRS
CO-PAY PROGRAM
AND
CASE MANAGEMENT AGENCIES

DIVISION OF ELDERLY AFFAIRS
HOME AND COMMUNITY CARE
CO-PAYMENT PROGRAM

For persons who meet the guidelines for the Division of Elderly Affairs Care Co-Payment Program, services are offered at a reduced rate to Rhode Island residents aged 65 and over and homebound. There are also annual income guidelines for single and married persons that will determine eligibility in the program. The guidelines change annually. Once eligible, the participants will pay a co-pay, which is determined by the participant's income.

Based on eligibility, these services may include home health aid services, adult day services, personal emergency response systems, meals, trans-portation, senior companions, minor home modifications, and minor assistive devices.

The Division of Elderly Affairs works with a network of regional Case Management Agencies to develop care plans and to determine eligibility for programs. A case manager will be assigned to perform an assessment and coordinate services for the participant. These plans help seniors re-main in their homes with a maximum independence.

Call the agency that services your community for more information, or call the Division of Elderly Affairs at 401-462-0570 or visit the following link: http://www.dhs.ri.gov/Programs/LTCHomeandCommunityBased.php.

The Following is a list of Case Management Agencies:

East Bay Community Action Program

www.ebcap.org

100 Bullocks Point Avenue
Riverside, Rhode Island 02915

Telephone: 401-437-1000

Communities Served: Bristol, Central Falls, East Bay, and Pawtucket

Child and Family Services of Newport

www.cfsnewport.org

31 John Clarke Road
Middletown, Rhode Island 02842
Telephone: 401-849-2300

Communities Served: Newport County

West Bay Community Action Program

www.westbaycap.org
224 Buttonwoods Avenue
Warwick, RI 02886   Phone: (401) 732-4660

Communities Served: Coventry, East Greenwich, Warwick, and West Warwick

Tri-Town Community Action Program

www.tri-town.org
1126 Hartford Avenue   Phone: (401) 351-2750
Johnston, RI 02919

Communities served: Providence County, Kent County, and Washington County

Providence Community Action Program

www.cappri.org
518 Hartford Avenue   Phone: (401) 273-2000
Providence, RI 02909

Communities served: Providence

South County Community Action Program

www.sccainc.org   Phone: (401) 789-3016 1935
Kingston Road
Peace Dale, RI 02879
Communities served: Charlestown, Exeter, Hopkinton, Narragansett,New Shoreham, North Kingstown, Richmond, South Kingstown, West Greenwich, and Westerly

Blackstone Valley Community Action Program

www.bvcap.org
32 Goff Avenue   Phone: (401) 723-4520
Pawtucket, RI 02860
Communities served: Central Falls, Cumberland, Lincoln, North Smith-field, Pawtucket, and Woonsocket.

Notes

HOME MODIFICATIONS

Staying in Your Home as You Age

By Steve St Onge

According to a recent AARP survey, the majority of seniors prefer to remain in their own homes for as long as possible. This trend is called 'Aging in Place'. But their homes, unless properly designed and equipped, will not be able to accommodate their changing levels of mobility, vision and needs.

Accessibility modifications allow people to remain in their homes as they age. *Amenities like walk-in showers, better lighting, grab rails, and other modifications allow seniors to live comfortably, safely and independently in their own home for as long as possible.*

Most homeowners don't wish to refer to their home as 'handicapped-accessible' - in fact, the industry term for this is now called 'Universal Design.' **This is a user-friendly approach to design where people of any age, size, and ability can live and move about the environment comfortably, safely and independently.** It incorporates such features as lever style door handles and faucets, accessible bathing facilities, adjustable or varying height sinks and countertops, wider doorways, and low thresholds - all using stylish products and techniques that avoid an institutional look.

The National Association of Home Builders (NAHB) and the AARP have developed a new designation called Certified Aging in Place Specialist (CAPS) to assist aging homeowners to identify reputable contractors that have been trained in Universal Design techniques and to understand the unique needs of our aging population. Staying at home is an option for aging seniors, especially if one plans ahead and makes the proper modifications to their homes.

To find a CAPS certified remodeler, go to www.NAHB.org and click on the CAPS link.

Is A Reverse Mortgage Right For You?

If you're a homeowner age 62 or older, a reverse mortgage could be right for you. Use the cash to supplement your retirement income, finance home renovations, or pay for long-term health care coverage. *For whatever is important to you.*

A reverse mortgage is a loan that allows senior homeowners to convert home equity into cash while living at home for as long as they want to. You can receive payments as a lump sum, line of credit, or monthly payment for a specific term or for life. **Funds are tax-free and may be used for** any purpose. Borrowers continue to own their own home. There is no monthly mortgage payment, income or credit qualifications, and the loan does not becomes due until the (last) borrower moves out, dies, or sells the home. Enjoy financial security and independence.

Reverse Mortgages "The Basics"

- A loan that allows homeowners, age 62 or older, to convert home equity into cash while living at home for as long as they want

- No income or full credit review

- Borrower can receive payments as a lump sum, line of credit, monthly payment for a specific term or for life. Funds are tax-free and can be used for any purpose

- Loan becomes due when the (last) borrower moves out, dies or sells the home

- Borrowers continue to own their own home

- *Home must be 1-4 family residence*

Reverse Mortgages "The Benefits"

- Allows assets to be liquidated without triggering tax events or requiring any debt service.

- Proceeds are not considered income and therefore are not taxable. Eligibility for Social Security or Medicare benefits are not affected.

- Loan is repaid at time of death, sale or move. Repayment never exceeds value of the home.

- Loan proceeds can be used for whatever is important to you.

- Independent counseling is required for all reverse mortgages

The "Borrowers Responsibility"

- Keep property taxes current

- Maintain homeowners insurance

- Maintain property in reasonable living condition

- Live in the home as primary residence

The "safety of A Home Equity Conversion Mortgage (HECM) Reverse mortgage"

- Federal Housing Authority administers the Home Equity Conversion Mortgage and guarantees that the borrower receive their requested loan advance.

- The borrower(s) will never owe more than the fair market value of the home upon loan maturity

- You can change your payment distribution at any time during the life of the loan.

The "Typical Closing Costs"

- Origination fee (2% of home value)

- Third party closing cost (appraisal, credit report, flood certificate, attorney fees)

- Mortgage Insurance Premium (2% of home value)

- Most fees can be paid from loan proceeds

- *Closing costs may be dramatically reduced with the fixed rate products*

SUBSIDIZED HOUSING &HOUSING ASSISTANCE

Rhode Island Housing and Subsidized Housing

44 Washington Street

Providence, RI 02903

Telephone: (401) 457 1234; TTY: (401) 450-1394

Rhode Island Housing oversees the management of 20,000 apartment for low-income seniors, frail seniors, and persons with disabilities. Approximately 15,000 of these apartment are Section 8. Under this category, tenants pay 30 percent of their income for rent. Many cities and towns have public housing authorities that provide affordable apartments and Section 8 vouchers. The remaining 5,000 apartments have a variety of subsidies that keep the rents affordable for low-income households. Applicant can apply for housing in any community in which they would like to live. Be prepared to find out that most communities do have long waiting lists.

Crossroads Rhode Island

www.crossroadsri.org

160 Broad Street

Providence, RI 02903

Telephone: (401) 521-2255; TTY: (401) 277-4381

Crossroads Rhode Island provides information and referrals for the homeless and those in transition.

Home Improvement Assistance & Lead Abatement Program

www.rhodeislandhousing.org

44 Washington Street

Providence, RI 02903

Telephone: (401) 450-1350

Rhode Island Housing's Home Improvement and Lead Abatement program can assist qualified residents in obtaining low-interest home repair and improve-ment loans.

- *There may also be grants or loans for home repairs available in your city or town. You should call your city or town housing authority or visit your town/city hall for more information.*

Operation Stand Down

www.osdri.org

1010 Hartford Avenue

Johnston, RI 02919

Telephone: (401) 383-4730

Operation Stand Down Rhode Island serves homeless and disabled veterans.

Rhode Island Coalition for the Homeless

www.rihomeless.org

160 Broad Street

Providence, RI 02903

Telephone: (401) 421-6458

The Rhode Island Coalition for the Homeless publishes he Street Sheet, a listing of emergency shelters, food pantries, and other resources.

HEATING ASSISTANCE

Low-Income Home Energy Assistance Program (LIHEAP)

Heating assistance is available to households that are responsible for their own heating costs. The Low-Income Home Energy Assistance Program provides heating assistance to income eligible customers in meeting the costs of keeping their homes warm in the winter months.

The amount of assistance provided is based on household size and income level. Current income guidelines can be found by visiting the following link: http://www.dhs.ri.gov/Programs/ FY2017LowIncomeGuidelines.php.

The following agencies can assist with applying for heating assistance (see communities served to locate which agency you should call):

Blackstone Valley Community Action Program

www.bvcap.org   Phone: (401) 723-0227
32 Goff Avenue
Pawtucket, RI 02860

Communities served: Central Falls, Cumberland, Lincoln, North Smithfield, Pawtucket, and Woonsocket.

Cranston Comprehensive Community Action Program

www.comcap.org
311 Doric Avenue
Cranston, RI 02910
                                       Phone: (401) 467-9610

Communities served: Cranston, Foster, and Scituate.

Housing Assistance Continued....

East Bay Community Action Program

*www.*ebcap.org

100 Bullocks Point Avenue   Phone: (401) 437-5102

Riverside, RI 02915

Communities served: Barrington, Bristol, East Providence, Jamestown, Little Compton, Middletown, Newport, Portsmouth, Tiverton, and Warren .

*

Tri-Town Community Action Program

*www.*tri-town.org

1126 Hartford Avenue   Phone: (401) 351-2750

Johnston, RI 02919

Communities served: Burillville, Chepachet, Glocester, Johnston, and North Providence.

*

Providence Community Action Program

*www.*procapri.org

518 Hartford Avenue   Phone: (401) 273-2000

Providence, RI 02909

Communities served: Providence

*

South County Community Action Program

1935 Kingston Road   Phone: (401) 789-3016

Peace Dale, RI 02879   *www.*sccainc.org

Communities served: Charlestown, Exeter, Hopkinton, Narragansett, New Shoreham, North Kingstown, Richmond, South Kingstown, West Greenwich, and Westerly.

Heating Assistance Continued....

Citizen's Energy

*www.*citizensenergy.com

The Citizen's Energy website provides a listing of energy assistance re-sources in Rhode Island.

Diocese of Providence

*www.*heatri.com   Phone: (401) 421-7833

184 Broad Street

Providence, RI 02903

The Diocese of Providence has a program call ***Keep the Heat On*** that provides heating assistance in emergency situations.

*

Salvation Army

www.use.salvationarmy.com

386 Broad Street   Phone: (401) 451-5270

Providence, RI 02903

The Salvation Army Rhode Island provides heating and utility assistance.

COMPANIONSHIP AT HOME

Neighborhood Friendly Visitor Program

1 Cathedral Square   Phone: (401) 421-7833 ext.4

Providence, RI 02903

The Neighborhood Friendly Visitor Program provides companionship and friendly support to individuals. Volunteers visit homebound individuals and offer the social contact every person needs in their life. The program welcomes volunteers who wish to volunteer some of their time to others. To find out about obtaining a visitor, simply call the numbers above.

*

Rhode Island's Senior Companion Program (401) 462-0569

The Senior Companion Program is sponsored by the Division of Elderly Affairs and is funded by the Corporation for National and Community Service. All volunteers are 60 and over, have limited income and receive a tax-free stipend and other benefits while serving clients 20 hours weekly.

The Volunteers serve isolated and older adults in their homes and other community sites, such as senior centers and adult day care centers. In an average week, Senior Companions visit with almost 500 individuals, offer-ing friendship and compassion to those in need.

*

Southern Rhode Island Volunteers: SRI

www.southernrivol.org

10 Park Lane   Phone: (401) 552-7661

Charlestown, RI

Southern Rhode Island Volunteers, also known as Seniors Helping Others, offers a range of services such as visitation and education, that enrich the lives of those in need, while also enriching the lives of the volunteers and the entire community. Call or visit the website for more information.

LIFELINE PERSONAL EMERGENCY RESPONSE SYSTEMS

Lifeline clients are supported 24 hours a day, seven days a week, by wearing a communicator button. When the button is pressed, the subscriber is connected to a Lifeline operator. From there, the operator will assess the situation and contact the appropriate help.

Lifeline also offers special units for clients with visual and/or hearing impairments.

For more information emergency response systems, contact the POINT at (401) 462-4444.

SENIOR CONTINUING EDUCATION OPPORTUNITIES

EDUCATIONAL OPPORTUNITIES

The Elderhostel Program

The Elderhostel Program is the world's largest travel and education organization for persons age 55 and older. The organization's focus is on education and lifelong learning adventures. Financial assistance is available to eligible participants.

For more information call 1-877-426-8056 or visit www.elderhostel.org.

The Osher Lifelong Learning Institute

The Osher Lifelong Learning Institute at the University of Rhode Island is a learning community for adults age 50 and older. *Participants can explore a broad range of subjects and programs without the worry of exams, grades, or academic requirements!* There is a $50 inaugural membership fee.

For more information call (401) 874-5331 or (401) 864-7846 or visit www.uri.edu/OLLI

Rhode Island State Colleges and Universities

Rhode Island residents age 60 and over may take courses at state colleges and universities, without paying tuition, on a space-available basis. Students must meet the income guidelines and other fees may apply. Contact the college/university office of continuing education for more information.

You are Never Too Old to Learn

SENIOR
CENTERS

WHAT IS A SENIOR CENTER?

Senior Centers are meeting places that are dedicated to helping seniors live meaningful lives of dignity, enjoyment, and useful purpose. The centers' main focus is improving and enriching lives of seniors through programs, resources, and volunteer work. They provide programs and services that enhance an individual's social, physical and mental well-being.

Each town typically has its own Senior Center for the surrounding community. Membership fees vary for town and non-town members but prices are generally minimal. Most centers provide their own transportation. Ask your community senior center for more specific transportation information.

Membership fees, hours, and availability of programs may vary by location. Call your center for more details and information. For your convenience, the following Senior Centers have been listed alphabetically by city/town.

Barrington:

Barrington Senior Center

www.CI.Barrington.RI.US

281 County Road

Barrington, RI 02806

Phone: (401) 247-1926

Fax: (401) 247-3790

Bristol:

Benjamin Church Senior Center

1020 Hope Street

Bristol, RI 02809

Phone: (401) 253-8458

Fax: (401) 253-8009

Central Falls:

Ralph J. Holden Community Center

361 Cowden Street

Central Falls, RI 02863

Phone: (401) 727-7425

Fax: (401) 727-7428

Charlestown:

Charlestown Community Center

www.CharlestownRI.org 100 Park Lane

Charlestown, RI 02813

Phone: (401) 364-9955

Fax: (401) 364-0330

Coventry:

The Coventry Senior Center

www.Town.Coventry.RI.US

50 Wood Street

Coventry, RI 02816

Phone: (401) 822-9175

Fax: (401) 822-9128

Cranston:

The Cranston Department of Senior Services

www.CranstonRI.com

1070 Cranston Street

Cranston, RI 02920

Phone: (401) 780-6000

Fax: (401) 946-5909

Cumberland:

The Cumberland Senior Center

www.CumberlandRI.org

1464 Diamond Hill Road

Cumberland, RI 02864

Phone: (401) 334-2555

Fax: (401) 335-4473

East Greenwich:

East Greenwich Senior Services

125 Main Street

East Greenwich, RI 02818

Phone: (401) 886-8669

Fax: (401) 886-8623

East Providence:

The East Providence Senior Center

www.CityOfEastProv.com

610 Waterman Avenue   Phone: (401) 435-7800

East Providence, RI 02914   Fax: (401) 435-7803

Glocester:

Glocester Senior Center

www.GlocesterRI.org / SeniorServices.htm

1210 Putnam Pike   Phone: (401) 710-9860

Chepachet, RI 02815

Hopkinton:
Hopkinton Senior Services
www.HopkintonRI.org

     Phone: (401) 377-7795

188A Main Street

Ashaway, RI 02804   Alternate: (401) 377-2857

     Fax: (401) 377-7756

Jamestown Senior Center
6 West Street   Phone: (401) 423-2658
Jamestown, RI 02835   Fax: (401) 423-3252

Johnston Senior Center   Phone: (401) 944-3343

1291 Hartford Avenue   Fax: (401) 944-3560

Johnston, RI 02919

Lincoln:

The Lincoln Senior Center

www.LincolnRI.org

150 Jenckes Hill Raod

Lincoln, RI 02865

Phone: (401) 753-7000

Fax: (401) 753-7070

Middletown:

The Middletown Senior Center

www.MiddletownRI.com/Senior

650 Green End Avenue

Middletown, RI 02842

Phone: (401) 849-8823

Fax: (401) 845-0411

Narragansett:

Narragansett Community Center

www.NarragansettRI.com

53 Mumford Road

Narragansett, RI 02882

Phone: (401) 782-0675

Fax: (401) 788-2565

Newport:

Edward King House

www.EdwardKingHouse.com

35 King Street

Newport, RI 02840

Phone: (401) 846-7426

Martin Luther King Center

www.MLKccenter.org

20 Dr. Marcus Wheatland Blvd.

Newport, RI 02840

Phone: (401) 846-4828

Fax: (401) 848-7360

North Kingstown:
Beechwood House Senior

Center *www.NorthKingstown.org/senior*

10 Beach Street

North Kingstown, RI 02852

Phone: (401) 294-3331

Fax: (401) 294-3020

North Providence:

Salvatore Mancini Center

w.smrac.com

2 Atlantic Boulevard

North Providence, RI 02911

Phone: (401) 231-0742

Fax: (401) 232-3460

Pawtucket:

Leon Mathieu Senior Center

Email: Mathieuctr@yahoo.com

420 Main Street

Pawtucket, RI 02860

Phone: (401) 728-7582

Fax: (401) 725-8220

Portsmouth:

The Portsmouth Multi Purpose Senior Center

www.PortsmouthRI.com

110 Bristol Ferry Road   Phone: (401) 683-4100

Portsmouth, RI 02871   Fax: (401) 683-4001

Providence:

DaVinci Community Center

www.DavinciCenter.org

470 Charles Street   Phone: (401) 272-7471

Providence, RI 02904   Fax: (401) 272-7960

Federal Hill Community Center   Phone: (401) 421-4722

9 Courtland Street   Fax: (401) 421-4725

Providence, RI 02909

Fox Point Senior Center   Phone: (401)751-2217

90 Ives Street   Fax: (401) 490-0699

Providence, RI 02906

Hamilton House

www.HistoricHamilton.com

276 Angell Street

Providence, RI 02906

Phone: (401) 831-1800

Fax (401) 331-1963

Hartford Park Senior Center

20 Syracuse Street

Providence, RI 02909

Telephone (401) 521-1180

Jewish Community Center

www.jccri.org / seniors

401 Elmgrove Avenue

Providence, RI 02906

Phone: (401) 861-8800

Fax: (401) 331-7961

Nickerson House Senior Center

133 Delaine Street

Providence, RI 02909

Phone: (401) 351-2241

Fax: (401) 272-3296

Silver Lake Center

529 Plainfield Street

Providence, RI 02909

Phone: (401) 944-8300

Fax: (401) 946-3260

St. Martin DePorres Senior Center

160 Cranston Street

Providence, RI 02907

Phone: (401) 274-6783

Fax: (401) 274-5930

Washington Park Community Center

42 Jillson Street

Providence, RI 02905

Phone: (401) 461-6650

Fax: (401) 781-5262

West End Community Center

109 Bucklin Street

Providence, RI 02907

Phone: (401) 781-4242

Fax: (401) 467-7990

Richmond Adult Center

1168 Main Street

Richmond, RI 02898

Phone: (401) 539-6144

Fax: (401) 491-9363

Scituate Senior Center

www.ScituateRI.org

1315 Chopmist Hill Road

North Scituate, RI 02857

Phone: (401) 647-2662

Fax: (401) 647-3160

Smithfield:

Smithfield Senior Center

www.SmithfieldRI.com/SeniorCenter.htm

1 William Hawkins, Jr. Trail   Phone: (401) 949-4590

Smithfield, RI 02828   Fax: (401) 949-4593

South Kingstown:

The Center

www.SouthKingstownRI.com

25 Saint Dominic Road   Phone: (401) 789-0268

Wakefield, RI 02879   Fax: (401) 782-1223

Tiverton:

Tiverton Senior Center

www.SeniorCenter@TownOfTivertonRI.com

207 Canonicus Street   Phone: (401) 625-6790

Tiverton, RI 02878   Fax: (401) 625-6793

Warren:

Warren Senior Center

www.Warren.RI.com

20 Libby Lane, Andreozzi Hall   Phone: (401) 247-1930

Warren, RI 02885   Fax: (401) 245-1392

Warwick:

JONAH Community Center

www.JonahCenterRI.com

830 Oakland Beach Avenue

Phone: (401) 739-1305

Warwick, RI 02889

Fax: (401) 732-3644

Pilgrim Senior Center

www.WarwickRI.gov

27 Pilgrim Parkway

Phone: (401) 468-4090

Warwick, RI 02888

Fax: (401) 468-4091

West Warwick:

West Warwick Senior Center

145 Washington Street

Phone: (401) 822-4450

West Warwick, RI 02893

Fax: (401) 828-2274

Westerly:

The Westerly Senior Citizens Center

www.WesterlySeniorCenter.org

39 State Street

Phone: (401) 596-2404

Westerly, RI 02891

Fax: (401) 596-4991

Woonsocket:

Woonsocket Senior Center

84 Social Street

Phone: (401) 766-3734

Woonsocket, RI 02895

Fax: (401) 765-5578

Notes

GERIATRIC CARE MANAGEMENT

WHAT IS A GERIATRIC CARE MANAGER?

A Geriatric Care Manager (GCM) is a professional with specialized knowledge and expertise in senior care issues. Sometimes called case managers, elder care managers, service coordinators or care coordinators, GCMs are individuals who evaluate your situation, identify solutions, and work with you to design a plan for maximizing your elder's independence and well being.

Geriatric care management usually involves an in-depth assessment, developing a care plan, arranging for services, and following up on monitoring care. While you are not obligated to implement any part of the suggested care plan, Geriatric Care Managers often suggest potential alternatives you might not have considered, due to their experience and familiarity with community resources. They can also make sure your loved one receives the best possible care and any benefits to which they are entitled.

Geriatric Care Managers receive a variety of training, from bachelor degrees to multiple doctorates in gerontology, social work, psychology, and nursing. The following are just a few examples of types of credentials.

BSN—Bachelor of Science in Nursing

MPH—Master of Public Health

RN— Registered Nurse

MSW— Masters in Social Work

MHSA— Mental Health/Substance Abuse

LSW— Licensed Social Worker

CMC— Care Manager, Certified

Health Touch, Inc.
626 Tollgate Road
Warwick, RI 02886

www.CNEHomeHealth.org
Phone: (401) 788-2400
Fax: (401) 788-9386

Care Partnering
108 Beardsworth Road
Tiverton, RI 02878

www.CarePartnering.com
Phone: (401) 559-5668
Email: mpmasse1@cox.net

Specialty Personnel Services, Inc.
790 Charles Street
Providence, RI 02904

www.SpecialtyPersonnelServices.com
Phone: (401) 455-0111
Fax: (401) 455-0220

Carmen M. Roy, *BSN, MPH, RN*
Elder at Home, LLC
75 East Avenue
Pawtucket, RI 02860

www.ElderAtHome.com
Phone: (401) 475-7705

NOTES AND NUMBERS

NOTES AND NUMBERS

GERIATRIC ASSESSMENTS

GERIATRIC ASSESSMENTS

Geriatric assessment units conduct comprehensive assessments of a person's medical status. Seniors who have shown recent changes in their physical, psychological, or social functioning are candidates for assessment. A team of professionals identifies health and medical problems and plans a course of treatment. These organizations offer geriatric assessments:

OUTPATIENT GERIATRIC ASSESSMENTS

Butler Hospital Memory and Aging Program
Providence, RI

Phone: (401) 455-6403

www.MemoryDisorder.org

Founded in 1997, this program is dedicated to developing new treatments that improve the quality of life for patients and families dealing with memory loss. Affiliated with Brown Medical School, the program's mission is to assist individuals with memory loss, and their families, by providing comprehensive assessments and the latest treatments. The work of the Memory and Aging Program includes extensive research studies to develop new treatments for memory loss.

RI Mood and Memory Research Institute

East Providence, RI

Phone: (401) 435-8950

www.RIMMRI.com

Rhode Island Mood and Memory Research Institute welcomes generally healthy individuals living with a disease or condition looking to improve their quality of life.

Dr. John Stoukides is the primary researcher at Rhode Island Mood and Memory Research Institute.

Clinical trials are open to all ages and each study has specific requirements. Study procedures, risks and benefits are explained by the study coordinator prior to participating in the study during the informed consent process.

Please visit us on Facebook for more information and Caregiver Tips!

Geriatrics and Palliative Medicine

Practice & Services

Serving all of Rhode Island

Phone: (401) 728-7270

Roger Williams Geriatric Consultation Service

North Providence, RI

Phone: (401) 231-0450

INPATIENT GERIATRIC ASSESSMENTS

Butler Hospital Senior Treatment Program

Providence, RI

Phone: (401) 455-6220

Butler Hospital's Senior treatment program offers a comprehensive approach to treating seniors who have depression, anxiety, or memory disorders, as well as patients who have cognitive disorders with complicating psychiatric behaviors. The Center's physicians are internationally recognized experts in caring for seniors with a dual diagnosis of a medical and a psychiatric illness and work along-side experienced nurses who are committed to working with older people affected by memory disorders and behavioral problems.

Roger Williams Medical Center Behavioral Health

Providence, RI

Phone: (401) 456-2363

Toll-Free: (800) 252-6466

Veterans Administration Mental Health

Providence, RI

Phone: (401) 457-3083

Notes

GERIATRIC PHYSICIANS

WHAT IS A GERIATRICIAN?

A Geriatrician is a medical doctor who specializes in the medical needs of seniors. All seniors should consult with a geriatrician for a geriatric assessment, even if they already have a family physician. A geriatric assessment is a comprehensive evaluation designed to optimize an older person's ability to enjoy good health, improve their overall quality of life, reduce the need for hospitalization or institutionalization and enable them to live independently for as long as possible.

Aman Nanda, M.D.

University Medical Foundation

407 East Avenue, Suite 110

Pawtucket, RI 02860

(401) 728-7270

David Fried, M.D.

Coastal Medical

1351 South County Trail

East Greenwich, RI 02818

(401) 884-0333

Lynn McNicoll, M.D.

University Medical Foundation

407 East Avenue, Suite 110

Pawtucket, RI 02860

(401) 728-7270

Nadia Mujahid, M.D.

University Medical Foundation

407 East Avenue, Suite 110

Pawtucket, RI 02860

(401) 728-7270

Syed R. Mehdi, M.D.

Landmark Primary Care

115 Cass Avenue

Woonsocket, RI 02895

(401) 765-3135

John Stoukides, M.D.

(Geriatrician) Roger Williams Senior

Health Associates 2 Atlantic Boulevard

North Providence, RI 02911

(401) 231-0450

Notes

Notes

GERIATRIC
NEUROLOGISTS

WHAT IS A GERIATRIC NEUROLOGIST?

As a Geriatric subspecialty, Geriatric Neurology focuses on neurological diseases and disorders that are common to older adults. The correct diagnosis of neurological disorders in older adults is difficult because signs of disease may mimic normal signs of aging. In addition, patients frequently have more than one neurological problem at a time. This subspecialty is the result of growing recognition that neurological conditions may present differently in middle or late life, and that the older adult may require different treatments than younger patients.

The most common geriatric neurology problems is memory loss and dementia. In addition, many other neurological disorders are more common with age including, stroke, Parkinson's disease, seizures, and gait disorders. The subspecialty of geriatric neurology focuses on evaluating and treating these common neurological conditions in older adults.

NORTHERN RI

Dennis Aumentado, M.D.

RI Neurology Group, Inc.

1065 Mendon Road

Woonsocket, RI 02895

(401) 762-0170

Alla Korennaya, M.D.

175 Nate Whipple Highway, Suite
203 **Cumberland**, RI 02864

(401) 658-3600

GREATER PROVIDENCE

Motasem Al-Yacoub, M.D.

Landmark Medical Center 115
Cass Street **Woonsocket**, RI
02895

(401) 722-7300

Joseph V. Centrofanti, M.D.

725 Reservoir Avenue, Suite 308

Cranston, RI 02910

(401) 944-9559

Norman M. Gordon, M.D.

East Side Neurology

450 Veterans Memorial Parkway/

Building 11 **East Providence**, RI 02914

(401) 431-1860

Fred Griffith, M.D.

East Side Neurology

450 Veterans Memorial Parkway/

Building 11 **East Providence**, RI 02914

(401) 431-1860

Gary L'Europa, M.D.

Neurohealth, Inc.

227 Centerville Road

Warwick, RI 02886

(401) 732-3332

Albert J. Marano, M.D.

1524 Atwood Avenue, Suite 244

Johnston, RI 02919

(401) 272-7660

❋

Thomas Morgan, M.D.

54 Jefferson Boulevard

Warwick, RI 02888

(401) 467-7720

❋

Brian R. Ott, M.D.

AD & Memory Disorders Center/ RI

Hospital Ambulatory Patient Center/

6th Floor

593 Eddy Street

Providence, RI 02903

(401) 444-6440

Stephen Salloway, M. D.

Memory and Aging Program/Butler

Hospital 345 Blackstone Boulevard

Providence, RI 02906

(401) 455-6403

Susan D. Weinman, M.D.

Long-term Care Psychiatry

345 Blackstone Boulevard/ Suite C-311

Providence, RI 02906

(401) 277-9935

EAST BAY

Elaine C. Jones, M. D. (Neurologist)

Southern New England Neurology

1180 Hope Street (Bristol Medical Center)

Bristol, RI 02809

(401) 289-0992

Randy B. Kozel, M.D. (Neurologist)

Aquidneck Neurology

10 King Charles Drive

Portsmouth, RI 02871

(401) 683-9002

Fax (401) 293-0330

✳

Brian R. Ott, M.D. (Neurologist)

Bristol Medical Center

1180 Hope Street

Bristol, RI 02809

(401) 253-8900

✳

Suzanne Patrick-Mackinnon, M.D.

(Neurologist) 244 East Main Road

Portsmouth, RI 02871

(401) 683-1048

Notes

Notes

ADULT
DAY CARE

WHAT IS ADULT DAY CARE?

Adult day care is a planned program of activities designed to promote well-being though social and health related services. Adult day care centers operate during daytime hours in a safe, supportive environment. Nutritious meals that accommodate special diets are typically included, along with an afternoon snack.

Adult day care centers can be public or private, non-profit or for-profit. The intent of an adult day care center is primarily two-fold:

1) To provide older adults an opportunity to get out of the house and receive both mental and social stimulation.

2) To give caregivers a much-needed break in which to attend to personal needs, or simply rest and relax.

Good candidates for adult day care are individuals who can benefit from the friendship and functional assistance a day care center offers, as well as individuals or that may be physically or cognitively challenged but do not require 24-hour supervision.

Adult day care center participants need to be mobile, with the possible assistance of a cane, walker or wheelchair, and in most cases, they must also be continent.

Common recreational activities include arts and crafts, musical entertainment, mental stimulation games, exercise, discussion groups, holiday and birthday celebrations, local outings, and inter-generational programs.

Some Adult Day Centers offer *shower services* for a small fee. Call the Day Center you are interested in to inquire. This can be a wonderful service to Caregivers having difficulty showering and bathing their loved one.

Besides recreational activities, some adult day care centers provide transportation to and from the center, social services including counseling and support groups for caregivers, and health support services such as blood pressure monitoring and vision screening. Often, adult day care centers provide health assessments and therapy if staffed with a Registered Nurse or other health professionals. Other types of adult day care provide social and health services specifically for individuals with Alzheimer's Disease (including early-onset) or other memory/dementia related disorders.

The cost for an adult day care center ranges but is typically set on a per day basis. Many facilities offer services on a sliding fee scale, meaning that what you pay is based on your income and ability to pay. Be sure to ask about financial assistance.

Hope Alzheimer's Center

25 Brayton Avenue

Cranston, RI 02920

Phone: (401) 946-9220

Fax: (401) 946-3850

www.HopeAlzheimersCenter.org

Contact: Ellen Grizzetti, President/
CEO

Hours of Operation:

Monday-Friday   7:45am-5:00pm
Saturday   9:00am-4:00pm

Hope Alzheimer's Center, one of only two adult day health centers in Rhode Island dedicated specifically for Alzheimer's disease, is a nationally recognized, nonprofit facility with a goal of creating "Brighter Hours, Fuller Days, Richer Lives" for people with Alzheimer's disease and other progressive memory disorders. Since its opening in 1995, Hope has helped more than 1,000 families postpone, or even forgo, the need for nursing home placement Participants of all ability levels can take part in a wide range of activities, including yoga, tai chi, art, music, chair tap dancing, cognitive fitness, pottery, baking, men's club and intergenerational programs, among others. Nurses provide close medical supervision, including administering medication, monitoring glucose, and performing routine health assessments. Staff can assist with daily tasks such as toileting, personal hygiene, and feeding as needed. The center also offers social services, care management, on-site hairdresser and podiatry care, and transportation assistance.

Cornerstone Adult Services, Inc., Bristol Center

172 Franklin Street

Bristol, RI 02809

Monday-Friday 7:30am-4:30pm

Phone: (401) 254-9629

Fax: (401) 254-1597

www.Cornerstone-RI.com

The Willows Adult Day Care

47 Barker Avenue

Warren, RI 02885

Monday-Friday 7:30am-4:30pm

Saturday 8:00am-4pm

Phone: (401) 245-2323

Fax: (401) 247-9030

NOTES AND NUMBERS

Cornerstone Adult Services, Inc., Alzheimer's Center

140 Warwick Neck Avenue

Warwick, RI 02889

Phone: (401) 739-2844

Fax: (401) 739-5388

www.Cornerstone-RI.com

Hours of Operation:

Monday-Friday 7:30am-6:00pm

Saturday 9:00am-5:00pm

Cornerstone Adult Services, Inc., Apponaug Center

3720 Post Road

Warwick, RI 02886

Phone: (401) 739-2847

www.Cornerstone-RI.com

Hours of Operation:

Monday-Friday 7:30am-4:30pm

NOTES AND NUMBERS

Cornerstone Adult Services, Inc., Coventry Center

60 Wood Street

Coventry, RI 02816

Phone: (401) 822-6212

www.Cornerstone-RI.com

Hours of Operation:

Monday-Friday 7:30-4:30pm

NOTES AND NUMBERS

Nancy Brayton Osborn Adult Day Center

115 East Main Road

Little Compton, RI 02837

Phone: (401) 592-0465

Fax: (401) 592-0467

Hours of Operation:

Monday-Friday 8:30am-2:30pm

The Nancy Brayton Osborn Center offers programs to help adults who have Alzheimer's Disease as well as those with a functional, emotional and/or developmental disability. The center offers recreational and social activities, assistance with activities of daily living, medication assessment and monitoring, respite time, and caregiver support services.

Participants: 15-20

NOTES AND NUMBERS

Alternative Adult Care

84 Social Street

Woonsocket, RI 02895

Phone:(401) 766-0516

Fax: (401) 765-5578

www.SeniorServicesri.org/AAC.htm

Hours of Operation: Monday-
Friday 7:30am-3:00pm

Jewish Seniors Agency of RI

100 Niantic Avenue

Providence, RI 02907

Phone: (401) 351-2440

Fax: (401) 421-5905

www.JSARI.org/DayCare

Hours of Operation:
Monday-Friday 7:30am-4:30pm

NOTES AND NUMBERS

Cranston Adult Day Services

1070 Cranston Street **Cranston**, RI
02920

Phone: (401) 780-6243

Fax: (401) 946-5909

rcastiglione@cransonri.com

Hours of Operation:

Monday-Friday 7:45am-5:00pm

Dora C. Howard Centre, Ltd.

715 Putnam Pike **Greenville**, RI

02828 Phone: (401) 949-3890

Fax: (401) 949-5666

www.DoraCHoward.com

Hours of Operation:

Monday-Friday 7:30am-5:00pm

NOTES AND NUMBERS

Fruit Hill Day Services for Elderly

399 Fruit Hill Avenue

North Providence, RI 02911

Phone: (401) 353-5805

Fax: (401) 353-4904

Hours of Operation:

Monday-Friday 8:00am-4:00pm

Generations Adult Health Center

267 Jenckes HIll Road

Smithfield, RI

Phone: (401) 725-6400

Fax: (401) 722-5916

www.GenerationsPrograms.com

Hours of Operation:

Monday-Friday   7:00am-5:00pm

Saturday: 8:30am-1:30pm

Sunday: 10:00am-3:00pm

NOTES AND NUMBERS

New Horizons Adult Day Center   Hours of Operation:

426 Main Street   Monday-Friday 7:30-5:00pm

Pawtucket, RI 02860

Phone: (401)727-0950

www.newhorizonsadc.org

NOTES AND NUMBERS

South Kingstown Adult Day Services

283 Post Road

Wakefield, RI 02879

Phone: (401) 783-8736

Fax: (401) 792-9609

Hours of Operation: Monday-Friday 8:30am-3:30pm

www.southkingstownri.com/code/snrsvc_daycare.cfm

Operated by the town of South Kingstown, The Adult Day Services Center provides an array of supportive services designed to increase the activities of daily living for older persons dependent upon continual family support and supervision. The program provides supervised supportive care for frail elderly persons to meet the needs of the functionally impaired individual. The program also provides respite and emotional support to caregivers.

Participants: 20

Westerly Adult Day Services

65 Wells Street

Westerly, RI 02891

Phone: (401) 596-1336

Fax: (401) 596-6186

www.WADSInc.com

Hours of Operation:

Monday-Friday: 7:30am-4:00pm

NOTES AND NUMBERS

LIVE AND LEARN
PROGRAMS

The Live and Learn Program is designed specifically for persons who have been diagnosed with ***early memory loss***. The program provides a social support system outside of the family. It helps to increase self-esteem, avoid isolation, and improves mental and physical fitness in a safe and secure environment. Current session are held as follows (call 401-421-0008 to confirm current times and locations) :

Tuesdays from **9:30am-11:30am** *at the Warwick Public Library;*

Wednesdays from **1:00pm-2:30pm** *in Providence at the East Side Mount Hope YMCA of Providence.*

Tuesdays from **10:00am-12:00pm** *at Middletown St Lucy's Church;*

Wednesdays from **9:30am-11:00am** *at the Woonsocket Public Library;*

Thursdays from **10:00**-12:00pm *at North Kingstown St. Francis de Sales Parish;*

An interview with a staff person is required to determine whether the program meets the applicant's needs. For further information about the Live and Learn Program please contact the Alzheimer's Association—Rhode Island Chapter at (401) 421-0008 or visit them online at www.alz.org/ri

<u>*Always call the Alzheimer Association to confirm date, time, and place of meeting, as this may change from time to time.*</u>

Notes

LEGAL PLANNING
&
LONG-TERM CARE

WHO NEEDS TO CONSIDER LONG-TERM CARE PLANNING?

The four primary sources for funding long-term care costs are private pay, long-term care insurance, Medicare, and Medicaid. Medicare is very limited, and most senior clients do not have, or cannot afford, long-term care insurance. With that said, almost everyone who needs an institutional level of care eventually relies on Medicaid for payment. This is true because the costs are catastrophic and there are very few people who can afford to private pay for an extended period of time, particularly without impoverishing a healthy spouse who may be living in the community.

Financial planners, accountants, those in the health field, as well as prospective clients, often ask us "when should someone think about long-term care planning?" Many people mistakenly believe that long-term care planning is completely financially driven. The truth is that anyone over the age of sixty, or handicapped, or with a progressive disease or other health issue, should be engaging in long -term care planning. Any senior who owns a home should consider planning. Married couples should be particularly careful to engage in advanced long-term care planning, so as not to impoverish the healthier spouse should long-term care be needed. Even younger people should engage in long-term care planning through the use of a proper long-term care insurance policy.

Finally, it is crucial to seek the advice of an attorney experienced in elder law and estate planning. All too often, clients come into our office and tell us, "I know I did something with the deed … but I don't know what." If this is the case in your situation, or for a client you know, the documents and transactions should be reviewed immediately.

Additionally, if transfers have been made in the past it is very important that enough funds were reserved to pay through any period of ineligibility for Medicaid, as a result of the transfer. It is never too late to do planning, however the options available, as well as the savings to the client, will be severely limited if the individual waits until crisis strikes.

MEDICARE BASICS

Medicare is a federal health insurance program that provides benefits to the elderly and the disabled. Medicare is an entitlement and is available to individuals who are age 65 or over, the disabled, and those with permanent kidney failure.

Individuals with disabilities who are eligible for Social Security Disability Income (SSDI) and receive SSDI for a 24 month period will also qualify for Medicare.

Individuals with end-stage renal disease qualify for Medicare three months after beginning renal dialysis.

Basically, Rhode Island Seniors who have Medicare have one of three parts: Part A, Part B, and Part D, which are described as follows:

Medicare Part A:

Part A provides coverage for hospitalization, home health care, skilled nursing facility care, and hospice care. Part A coverage is offered at no charge to persons age 65 and older who are entitled to receive Social Security and Railroad Retirement benefits. Those age 65 and older not entitled to receive Social Security may "buy-in" to Medicare by paying a premium. Disabled individuals eligible for Medicare receive Part A benefits free of charge.

Medicare Part B:

Part B provides coverage for physician's services, diagnostic test, medical equipment, ambulance services, certain home care, and physical and speech therapy. Unlike Part A benefits, Part B requires the payment of a premium for all beneficiaries. Usually, this is automatically deducted from an individual's monthly Social Security income check.

Medicare Part D:

Part D provides beneficiaries with assistance with paying for prescription drugs. Part D coverage is not provided within the traditional Medicare program. Beneficiaries must enroll in one of many Part D plans offered by private companies.

For more information on Medicare health coverage, contact The Centers for Medicare and Medicaid Services (CMS) at www.cms.gov or call 1-800-MEDICARE. The mission of the CMS is to ensure effective, up-to-date health coverage.

MEDICAID BASICS

There are many different Medicaid Programs in Rhode Island that apply to seniors. There are programs that pay for care at home, in assisted living residences, in nursing homes, and adult day care centers.

Medicaid is different than Medicare because Medicare is an entitlement. Also, Medicare does not pay for custodial care in a nursing home; Medicare pays for a short period while a patient is rehabilitating (See the Medicare section for more information).

Rhode Island Institutional Medicaid rules will require that individuals meet the following tests, in addition to other state specific requirements:

1. **Citizenship:** An applicant for Institutional Medicaid must be a United States Citizen or a "qualified alien" (a permanent resident, an asylee, a refugee, a person paroled into the United States for at least a year, or a person granted conditional entry).

2. **Residence:** An Applicant must be a resident of the state where the application is being made.

3. **Medical Need**: The state will perform a medical evaluation of the applicant to qualify the applicant as needing long-term care.

4. **Resource Requirements**: Rhode Island requires that an applicant have available resources worth less than $4,000. The spouses of married applicants are also limited as to what resources they may keep.

5. **Income Requirements:** States vary, but in Rhode Island Income eligibility is met by the inability to the pay the actual cost of private care with available income.

Prior to applying for Medicaid, it is very important that the applicant and/or her family seek advice as to eligibility. Uniformed and misinformed applicants often apply for benefits and are denied for various reason, the following being the most popular reasons:

1. Resource requirements have not been met.

2. Assets were given away in order to qualify for Medicaid and the application was made during a period of ineligibility.

The spouse of a married applicant must be proactive in getting correct legal advice from an elder law attorney familiar with Rhode Island law, so as to not become impoverished by the institutionalized spouse's long-term care costs.

Not all nursing homes participate in the Medicaid program. Therefore, it is crucial that families ask the facility of choice whether or not they do participate in Medicaid. If the facility does not participate in the Medicaid program, the resident will need to be relocated once his/her private funds are exhausted.

An elder law attorney can provide clients with advice which will vary depending on the laws in place at the time, as well as the client's individual scenario. Resolutions and techniques that are appropriate in Rhode Island may not be appropriate in other states.

By Laura M. Krohn, Attorney at Law, Author

To schedule an appointment with Laura please call:

401-398-8383

Laura M. Krohn Elder Law Attorney , Inc.
25 South County Commons Way
South Kingstown, Rhode Island 02879

www.seniorguideri.com

RI Durable Power of Attorney: Financial & Real Estate Matters

In many situations, family members or others will need to handle the financial affairs of a loved one. This could range from a single banking transaction to completing a Medicaid application, to selling a house.

To do so, the individual while competent, must have given such person written authority to make decisions on his or her behalf. The usual way this is done is through a document known as a "Durable Power of Attorney". If the Power of Attorney is "Durable" it will continue to be effective even if the person who executed the document becomes incapacitated. The person who signs the Durable Power of Attorney is known as the "principal." The person to whom the power is granted is known as the "agent" or "attorney-in-fact."

A properly drafted Durable Power of Attorney will give the power to gift to the agent, while including language that protects the principal while alive, as well as respects the principal's testamentary objectives.

Failure to execute a Durable Power of Attorney authorizing another to make decisions for you after your incapacity may mean that a court must be asked to appoint someone to assist. This is known as a "guardianship proceeding" and results in substantial legal expense and invasion of privacy.

When choosing an agent, this author always advises clients to choose a person(s) with a strong sense of integrity, who is responsible financially, and who respects and is familiar with the values and objectives of the client. It is a powerful document, which is not reviewed or regulated by any agency. Therefore the potential for abuse by agents under the Power of Attorney is great.

The sufficiency of most Power of Attorney forms is usually tested only after it is too late to make necessary revisions. When having this document prepared for a senior, a professional experienced in elder law issues should be consulted.

How to apply for Long-Term Care Medicaid

The Rhode Island Department of Human Services, the Executive Office of Health and Human Services, and HealthSource RI worked together to design Rhode Island's new, state-of-the-art eligibility system. This web-based system determines eligibility for Medicaid, Human Services Programs, and other forms of affordable health-care coverage using a single, streamlined application.

A Medicaid application may be submitted on-line or you can print a hard copy by visiting
www.dhs.ri.gov.

Nursing Home Transition Program

If you are both medically and financially eligible for Long-Term Care Medicaid, you may be able to receive those services in the home. This will not be 24/7, however it can be up to 50 or more hours per week. The only cost to the applicant is a portion of the applicant's income. Of course, it must cost less to provide the care in the home than it would in the nursing home.

If you are not in a nursing home, then you submit the Medicaid application along with the necessary medical verifications support-ing the need for the "highest" level of care. If you are in a nursing home, the Nursing Home Transition Program provides support and services to make the transition.

For more information on the Nursing Home Transition Program call 401-462-6393.

RI DURABLE POWER OF ATTORNEY: HEALTH CARE

An advanced directive is a written document executed by an individual which expresses that individual's health care decisions, including end of life decisions. A health care power of attorney is a document that the individual (referred to as the "Principal") uses to appoint a person (referred to as the "Representative" or "Health Care Agent") to make health decisions in the event the Principal becomes incapacitated. One form can be used for both purposes:

(1) to state a person's advanced health care decisions, and

(2) to appoint a representative.

All states have statutes that deal with a person's ability to make advanced directives. The Rhode Island legislature specifically states that adult persons have the fundamental right to control the decisions relating to the rendering of their own medical care. The Rhode Island legislature also declares the right of an adult person to make a written durable power of attorney for health care decisions and provides a statutory Health Care Power of Attorney form. The Rhode Island statutory Health Care Power of Attorney does provide an opportunity for an individual to state his or her advanced health care decisions.

Many individuals spend all or part of the year in another state, whether for vacation, medical reasons, or to visit family or friends. It is important to know that state laws are not uniform. Therefore, individuals that fall into this category should consider drafting a second health care power of attorney that complies with the law of the second state. Rhode Island will recognize a Power of attorney executed in another state, so long as it is executed in compliance with the laws of that state.

Finally, the choice of a health care representative is a very important decision. The representative should be someone who will honor the Principal's wishes and not be guided by their own wishes. That requires a person who will be emotionally strong and unwavering during times of medical crisis. This author strongly advises that only one health care representative be appointed at a time and always avoid the appointment of joint or co-representatives. The objectives behind executing advanced directives and health care power of attorney documents is to ensure that the health care decisions of the individual executing the document(s) are honored and that litigation is avoided.

Notes

WHEN IT IS TIME TO LEAVE HOME:

WHAT ARE THE OPTIONS?

INDEPENDENT LIVING
ASSISTED LIVING
& NURSING HOME CARE

SCANDINAVIAN
www.ScandinavianHome.com

Rehabilitation & Skilled Nursing

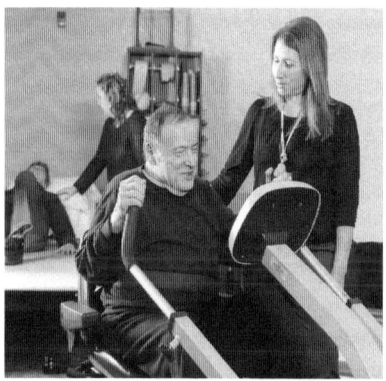

1811 Broad Street
Cranston, RI 02905

401-461-1433

♦ Short Term Rehab
♦ Respite Care
♦ Long Term Care
♦ End of Life Care

Assisted Living Community

50 Warwick Avenue
Cranston, RI 02905

401-461-1444

♦ Respite Suites
♦ Spacious One Bedroom
  Apartments
♦ Shared Apartments

A Non-profit Organization   *Care*Link Member

Our mission is to provide a continuum of excellent, compassionate and
innovative care to enable those we serve to obtain wellness and quality of life.

The Villa at Saint Antoine
400 Mendon Road
North Smithfield, RI 09896

www.stantoine.net
P: (401) 767-2574
F: (401) 767-2581

The Villa at Saint Antoine, the ultimate in assisted living, offers older adults a continuum of care in a tranquil and lovely community, under the auspice of the Diocese of Providence, adhering to tradition and excellence of care. Seniors realize their fullest potential and highest level of independence through the support of compassionate professionals providing detailed attention to meet their medical, social, emotional, and spiritual needs. Its gracious French country setting is beautifully designed and decorated to delight the senses while residents and their families enjoy an atmosphere graced by services and amenities comprising of healthy gourmet meals, assistance with activities of daily living, medication administration, 24 hours nursing care, housekeeping, transportation, wellness programs, social outings, respite suites, trial stays, and spiritual offerings – including in-house chaplain and daily mass. The MEZZANINE at the Villa is an innovative memory care unit offering patient centered services to residents with mild memory loss. All residents have priority access to specialized care including those offered at the Saint Antoine Residence - located in the same campus - for short-term rehabilitation, skilled nursing, or long-term care. The Villa is a non-profit organization that welcomes all seniors without regard to religious affiliation.

Veterans Aid & Attendance

Rehabilitation

Respite

Chapel

Pets

Salon

Saint Antoine Residence
10 Rhodes Avenue
North Smithfield, RI 09896

www.stantoine.net
P: (401) 767-3500
F: (401) 769-5249

Established in 1913, the Saint Antoine Residence is a 260 beds skilled nursing and rehabilitation facility located near I-295 and Route 146 in Northern Rhode Island. The community is a non-profit organization under the auspice of the Diocese of Providence and it adheres to the mission and long tradition of caring for the sick, the elderly, and their families by providing excellent care by compassionate professionals. Great attention is utilized to meet and exceed all expectations in regard to the emotional, physical, mental, and spiritual well being of its residents. Among its services and amenities, residents enjoy transitional care unit, 24 hour skilled nursing care, short term rehabilitation, long term care, secured dementia care unit, in-patient hospice suite, dietary services - including selective menus and therapeutic diets, activities and recreational programs, physician services, and spiritual care - including in-house chaplain and daily mass. Saint Antoine Residence is part of a continuum of care campus located in a beautiful and picturesque country setting adjacent to the Villa at Saint Antoine, a lovely on-site assisted living facility. The Residence welcomes all seniors without regard to religious affiliation.

Rehabilitation

Chapel

Salon

Medicaid

Secured Unit

ASSISTED LIVING RESIDENCE
884-9099
www.TheSeasons.org

The Seasons East Greenwich is a non-profit assisted living and memory-impaired care residence founded by the Scandinavian Home and Steere House Nursing and Rehabilitation Center. The residence offers 64 private, unfurnished studio, one bedroom and two bedroom apartments with private bath and kitchenette for traditional assisted living residents. Grandview Gardens, our memory care neighborhood, offers 20 private studio apartments with private bath.

Residents are offered a full range of assisted living services including three meals daily, bathing and dressing assistance, medication administration, housekeeping, and laundry.

Transportation to medical appointments is also offered. Activities are scheduled to enhance residents' independence and social, recreational, cultural, physical and spiritual needs. Through The Seasons founding members, residents benefit from priority consideration to two of the state's finest nursing homes.

Page 107

Tockwotton on the Waterfront
500 Waterfront Drive
East Providence, Rhode Island 02914
(401) 272-5280

Tockwotton on the waterfront is a community of uncompromising quality and comfortable surroundings where superior care is delivered by trusted professionals. This quality speaks to the mission of Tockwotton so rooted in the history of Providence, since its inception in 1856. Now situated on more than six acres of waterfront property in East Providence, Tockwotton on the Waterfront stays true to its mission. As a non-profit organization, we provide all of Rhode Island with a variety of services designed to meet the changing needs of older adults and their families. Services offered include the River's Edge Assisted Living, the Courtyard Memory Care, Short-Term Rehabilitation, and Long-Term Care, and Skilled Nursing. Tockwotton on the Waterfront is where a tradition of excellence meets waterfront elegance. Feel free to call us for a tour of our residence.

What Is Independent Living?

Independent Living provides the greatest flexibility and freedom among the many senior housing options available. Independent Living for seniors refers to residence in a compact, easy-to-maintain, private and personal apartment or house within a community of other seniors.

Seniors who decide on Independent Living generally must be healthy and able to manage their homes and personal needs on their own. Those choosing Independent Living simply must have a strong desire to take care of themselves, live independently and be able to communicate with doctors and caregivers on their own.

The housing arrangement is designed exclusively for seniors, generally those aged 55 and older. Typically, services such as meals, activities and transportation are included in a monthly fee. These fees are usually dependent upon the local market. Some subsidized senior Independent Living housing supply financial assistance to those seniors with limited incomes.

Independent Living for seniors is also known as Retirement Communities, Retirement Homes, Senior Apartments, Senior Housing, and Independent Living Communities. It is very important seniors choosing to live independently are willing to reach out for assistance on their own accord.

For additional information regarding the availability at, or amenities of an Independent Living community, call the community's main number and ask for the Director of Community Relations, or for the Admissions Director.

WHAT IS ASSISTED LIVING?

An assisted living residence provides care for seniors who need some help with activities of daily living yet wish to remain as independent as possible. Essentially, assisted living is the middle ground between independent living and nursing homes. The goal of assisted living is to provide seniors with an environment that encourages as much autonomy as they are capable of, while providing socialization, safety, and family peace of mind. Most residences offer 24-hour supervision and an array of support services, with more privacy, space, and dignity than many nursing homes, and at a lower cost. Assisted Living Residences are also called personal care homes, residential care facilities, domiciliary care, sheltered housing, and community residences.

An Assisted Living Residence helps seniors with personal care/custodial care, such as bathing, dressing, toileting, eating, grooming and transport. Daily contact with supervisory staff is the defining characteristic of an Assisted Living Residence. Medical care is usually limited in an Assisted Living Residence, but it is possible to contract for other medical needs.

Assisted Living Residences are owned and operated by both for-profit and non-profit organizations and can range in cost depending on where you live. Fees may be inclusive or there may be additional charges for special services.

Costs are generally lower than full-time home health services or nursing home care. Payment options will depend on the individuals situation, and may include private-pay, long-term care insurance, and Medicaid.

For additional information regarding the availability at, or amenities of an Assisted Living community, call the community's main number and ask for the Director of Community Relations, or for the Admissions Director.

What Is A Nursing Home & Rehabilitation Center?

A Nursing Home provides 24 hour care to people who can no longer care for themselves due to physical, emotional, or mental conditions. A licensed physician supervises each patient's care and a nurse or other medical professional is almost always on the premises. Most nursing homes have two basic types of services: skilled medical care and custodial care.

Skilled medical care includes services of trained professionals that are needed for a limited period of time following an injury or illness. This may include would care, I.V. administration and monitoring, physical therapy, speech therapy, occupational therapy, or administering and monitoring I.V. antibiotics for a severe infection. Skilled care may also be needed on a long term basis if a resident requires injections, ventilation or other similar treatment.

Custodial or personal care includes assistance with what are known as the activities of daily living. These include bathing, dressing, eating, grooming, transport, and incontinence care. This type of care may be a temporary or long-term need depending on the situation.

Nursing Homes/Skilled Nursing Facilities offer an array of services, in addition to the basic skilled nursing care and the custodial care. They provide a room (private or semi-private), all meals, some social activities, personal care, 24-hour nursing supervision and access to medical services when needed. In addition, many Nursing Homes provide respite care so that caregivers can have a break, and interim medical care which is care after a hospital stay.

ELDER ABUSE

THE DUTY TO REPORT ABUSE AND SELF-NEGLECT

TITLE 42
State Affairs and Government

CHAPTER 42-66
Elderly Affairs Department

SECTION 42-66-8

§ 42-66-8 Abuse, neglect, exploitation and self-neglect of elderly persons – Duty to report. – Any person who has reasonable cause to believe that any person sixty (60) years of age or older has been abused, neglected, or exploited, or is self-neglecting, shall make an immediate report to the director of the department of elderly affairs, or his or her designee, or appropriate law enforcement personnel. In cases of abuse, neglect, or exploitation, any person who fails to make the report shall be punished by a fine of not more than one thousand dollars ($1,000). Nothing in this section shall require an elder who is a victim of abuse, neglect, exploitation or who is self-neglecting, to make a report regarding such abuse, neglect, exploitation, or self-neglect to the director or his or her designee or appropriate law enforcement personnel.

History of Section.
(P.L. 1981, ch. 69, § 2; P.L. 1988, ch. 304, § 1; P.L. 1991, ch. 253, § 1; P.L. 2007, ch. 84, § 1; P.L. 2007, ch. 209, § 1; P.L. 2014, ch. 277, § 2; P.L. 2014, ch. 333, § 2.)

FACT:

- In 2003, two of every three elder-abuse victims were women and 43.7% were age 80 or older.

- A 2004 study found that 89.3% of elder abuse takes place in a domestic setting.

- Only 1 in 14 incidents of elder physical abuse that occurs in domestic settings is ever reported to the police.

- Types of elder maltreatment substantiated, include self neglect (37.2%), caregiver neglect (20.4%), emotional, psychological or verbal abuse (14.8%), financial exploitation (14.7%), physical abuse (10.7%), and sexual abuse (1%).

- Only 1 in 25 cases of elder financial exploitation is ever reported.

- Three of every four perpetrators of elder abuse and neglect are under 60 years of age.

- Most alleged offenders are adult children (32.6%) or other family members (21.5%). Spouses or other intimate partners account for 11.3% of the total.

NURSING HOME ABUSE, NEGLECT AND MISTREATMENT: WHAT TO LOOK FOR

Nursing Home Abuse

Bedsores, broken bones, malnutrition, dehydration, and other injuries suffered in nursing homes may be signs of abuse, neglect or mistreatment. Those signs may include unexplained bruises, cuts, burns, sprains, or fractures in various stages of healing; unexplained venereal disease or genital infections; and staff refusing to allow visitors to see a resident, or delays in allowing visitors to see the resident.

Nursing Home Neglect

Nursing home neglect is a general term that covers many different kinds of injuries. Falls, bedsores, elopement, dehydration, malnutrition, and choking on food are all signs of resident neglect.

Bedsores

The areas of the body at greatest risk for developing bedsores are the coccyx, hips, heels, and elbows. The most common cause is when an immobile nursing home resident is not repositioned or turned on a regular basis.

Side Rails and Bed Injuries

Side rails extend either the full length of the bed or part way. Most can be raised or lowered. Side rails are divided with slats spaced about six or more inches apart. This space can trap an elderly person's head, causing him or her to strangle. Often mattresses fit loosely in the frame, leaving gaps large enough to trap the resident between the mattress and side rail, also leading to suffocation and death.

Falls and Fractures

Falls are the most frequent cause of bone fractures among the elderly. Fractures can lead to serious health conditions, such as a difficulty in clearing the chest by coughing (which can lead to pneumonia), a loss of appetite, bedsores, and infections. 25% of elderly who sustain a hip fracture die within 6 months of the injury.

Dehydration

Since elderly persons often have a reduced sense of thirst, dehydration is one of the most frequent causes of hospitalization after age 65. Elderly dehydration is a serious health condition which can lead to death.

Malnutrition

Malnutrition, like dehydration, is a serious health problem among the elderly. Since the elderly have a reduced sense of taste and appetite, proactive steps may be required to prevent physical decline and wrongful death due to starvation.

Wandering/Elopement

Wandering by an elderly person with dementia or Alzheimer's can be a life-threatening situation. The elderly may wander into unsafe areas and be injured or killed. The most dangerous form of wandering is elopement in which the confused person leaves the protected area of the nursing home or assisted living residence and does not return.

Medication Errors

According to an article in the Boston Globe, nearly one out of every 10 nursing home residents suffers a medication-related injury each month. The risk of medication errors is much higher in nursing homes and assisted living residences than in hospital settings due to chronic understaffing.

Choking and Suffocation

Many nursing homes fail to assist or monitor residents, and the tragic result is a high number of deaths due to choking and suffocation. Much like children, many elderly persons who suffer from dementia or Alzheimer's need assistance with eating so they do not put too much food in their mouth at once. Other deaths can be caused by strangulation from restraints.

Physical and Sexual Assault

Sexual assault statistics indicate the widespread problem of rape and sexual assaults in nursing homes and assisted living residences. In legal terms, sexual assault includes any forced sexual contact that can range from unwanted touching to sexual penetration. The impact left because of sexual assault can be physically, psychologically and emotionally damaging.

DIVISION OF ELDERLY AFFAIRS PROTECTIVE SERVICES

Phone: (401) 462-0555

The DEA Protective Services Unit is responsible for investigating complaints of elderly abuse of Rhode Islanders 60 years of age and older by a family member, caregiver or person with duty of care. Abuse may include physical, emotional, sexual, financial exploitation, or abandonment.

Rhode Island law requires any person who has reasonable cause to believe that an elderly person has been abused to report it to DEA. Failure to report abuse of a person 60 years of age or older can result in a fine of up to $1,000.

The DEA Protective Services Unit develops a care plan to prevent additional abuse and address the elder's social service needs.

Self-Neglect occurs when a person is no longer able to care for himself/ herself. Reports of self-neglect are also made to the DEA Protective Services Unit. The senior's needs are assessed and necessary services are offered.

Under Rhode Island law, DEA records pertaining to a person reported to be abused, neglected, exploited or abandoned are confidential and are not deemed public records.

To file an elderly abuse or self-neglect report, call the Division of Elderly Affairs Protective Services Unit at (401) 462-0555.

ELIZABETH BUFFUM CHACE CENTER

Post Office Box 9476

Warwick, Rhode Island 02889

Business Phone: (401) 738-9700

24 Hour Crisis Hotline: (401) 738-1700

Fax: (401) 738-1713

Advocacy, support and protection for victims of domestic violence.

Confidential

- Staffed 24 hours a day by advocated trained to provide information, referrals, support, and individual safety plans for women or men victimized in a relationship.

- Short-term safe, confidential shelter for women and children in danger.

- No caller Identification

- All phone lines are blocked to ensure confidentiality

- Counseling and Support Groups

- Assistance at Police Departments

- Court advocates available to assist victims of domestic violence

ALL SUPPORT SERVICES ARE FREE OF CHARGE

NO ONE DESERVES ABUSE.

HELP IS AVAILABLE.

THE ALLIANCE FOR BETTER LONG TERM CARE
www.alliancebltc.com

Telephone (401) 785-3340 or 1-800-351-0808

The Alliance, as a non-profit, independent advocacy organization, ***defends the rights of those who can no longer speak for themselves - elderly and disabled Rhode Islanders who receive long term care services in nursing homes, assisted living residences, and those who receive licensed home care or hospice services.*** Residents in nursing homes are among the most frail and vulnerable. At times, they need help to improve their quality of life and care. An ombudsman can provide assistance so all facility residents receive respectful and competent care.

Rhode Island Coalition Against Domestic Violence

www.ricadv.org

24 Hour Hotline: 1-800-494-8100

Telephone: (401) 467-9940

The Rhode Island Coalition Against Domestic Violence works to eliminate domestic violence in Rhode Island. Its mission is to support and enhance the work of its member agencies and to provide leadership on the issue of domestic violence. The Coalition has a 24 Hour hotline. Additionally, the Coalition has published a **"Guide to Living Safely for Older Adults"**. Call 401-467-9940 to obtain a Guide.

Senior Citizen Police Advocates are police officers that are designated to make changes on the behalf of senior citizens regarding state legislature, specifically in cases of abuse and in dealing with elderly violators. The following is the most recent list. Always call for current advocate.

Town	Advocate	Telephone
Barrington	Kristy Viveros	437-3930
Block Island	Vincent Carlone	466-3220
Bristol	Adam Clifford/Russell Wood	253-6900
Burrillville	Brian Pitts	568-6255
Central Falls	Eileen Crenshaw	727-7411
Charlestown	Kevin Ryan	364-1212
Coventry	David Fraatz	826-1100
Cranston	Lori Sweeney	477-5073
Cumberland	David Payson	333-2500
East Greenwich	John Carter	884-2244
East Providence	Thomas Aguia	435-7630
Exeter	William Jamieson	444-1068
Foster	William Ziehl	397-3317
Glocester	Kimberly Bertholic	568-2533
Hopkinton		377-7750
Jamestown	James Chazes	423-1212
Johnston	Troy Maddocks	231-4210
Lincoln	Russell Enos	333-1111
Little Compton	Sue Cressman	635-2311
Middletown	David Gueriero	846-1144
Narragansett	Paula Boisclair	789-1091
North Kingstown	Todd Duchala	294-3316
Newport		847-1302
North Providence	Michael Tauarozzi	233-1433
North Smithfield	Sharon Pagliarini	762-1212

Town	Advocate	Telephone
Pawtucket	Joel Jarvia	727-9100
Portsmouth	Brett Bucholz	683-0300
Providence	William Merandi	243-6407
Richmond	Elwood Johnson	539-8289
Scituate	Donald Delaere	821-5900
Smithfield	Orlando Braxton/ Robert Squillante	231-2500
South Kingstown	Mark Healy	783-3321
Tiverton	Daniel Raymond	625-6716
Warren	Roy Vorges	245-1311
Warwick	Matthew Morretti	468-4325
Westerly	Tony Alicchio	596-2022
West Greenwich	Richard Brown	397-7191
West Warwick	John Randall	821-4323
Woonsocket	Matthew Ryan	766-1212
State Police	Joseph Meich	444-1000

Notes

Notes

HOSPITALS

Bradley Hospital

1011 Veterans Memorial Parkway
East Providence, RI 02915

Phone: (401) 432-1000
www.LifeSpan.org/Bradley

Butler Hospital

345 Blackstone Boulevard
Providence, RI 02906

Phone: (401) 455-6200
www.Butler.org

Eleanor Slater Hospital

14 Harrington Road
Cranston, RI 02920

Phone: (401) 462-2319
www.MHRH.RI.gov/ESH

Hasbro Children's Hospital

593 Eddy Street
Providence, RI 02903

Phone: 401-444-4000
www.LifeSpan.org/HCH

Kent Hospital

455 Toll Gate Road
Warwick, Rhode Island 02886

Phone: (401) 737-7000
wwww.KentHospital.org

Landmark Medical Center

115 Cass Avenue
Woonsocket, RI

Phone: (401) 769-4100
www.LandmarkMedical.org

Memorial Hospital of RI

111 Brewster Street
Pawtucket, RI 02860

Phone: (401) 729-2000
www.MHRIweb.org

The Miriam Hospital

164 Summit Avenue

Providence, RI 02906

Phone: (401) 793-2500

www.LifeSpan.org/TMH

Newport Hospital

11 Friendship Street

Newport, RI 02840

Phone: (401) 846-6400

www.LifeSpan.org/Newport

Our Lady of Fatima Hospital

200 High Service Avenue

N. Providence, RI 0290

Phone: (401) 456-3000

www.FatimaHospital.com

Rehabilitation Hospital of RI

116 Eddie Dowling Highway

N. Smithfield, RI 02896

Phone: (401) 766-0800

www.RHRI.net

Rhode Island Hospital

593 Eddy Street

Providence, RI 02903

Phone: (401) 444-4000

www.LifeSpan.org/RIH

Roger Williams Medical Center

825 Chalkstone Avenue

Providence, RI 02908

Phone: (401) 456-2000

www.RWMC.org

South County Hospital

100 Kenyon Avenue

Wakefield, RI 0287

Phone: (401) 782-8000

www.SCHospital.com

St. Joseph Hospital for Specialty Care

21 Peace Street   Phone: (401) 456-3000

Providence, RI 02904   *www.SpecialtyCareRI.com*

The Westerly Hospital

25 Wells Street   Phone: (401) 596-6000

Westerly, RI 02891   *www.WesterlyHospital.org*

Women & Infants Hospital

101 Dudley Street   Phone: (401) 274-1100

Providence, Rhode Island 02905   *www.WomenAndInfants.org*

Notes

HOSPICE CARE

WHAT IS HOSPICE?

Hospice is a specialized type of care that is designed to provide the patient and the family with th physical, emotional, and spiritual resources and support during their time of need. Hospice does not mean the patient is giving up on life. Instead, it means the focus is on comfort instead of cure to provide the best quality of life for as long as possible.

To qualify for hospice services the patient must have a life-limiting illness such as cancer, heart disease, stroke, end-stage Alzheimer's or any other condition with a life expectancy of less than six months.

Hospice covers the care as well as the cost and delivery of medical equipment, medications, and supplies. Most Hospice services are covered by Medicare, Medicaid, and private insurance. However, the services are always available regardless of ability to pay.

Hospice care is provided by a team with special training in end-of-life care and includes physicians nurses, social workers, spiritual counselors, and aids.

HOSPICE PROVIDERS

Kindred Hospice

www.kindredhospice.com

Telephone (401) 738-1492

Hope Hospice and Palliative Care

www.hopehospiceri.org

Telephone (401) 415-4200

Beacon Hospice, Inc.

www.beaconhospice.com

Telephone (877) 242-8394

VNA of Rhode Island Hospice

www.hospicevnari.org

Telephone (401) 574-4900

VNA of Care New England

www.vnacarenewengland.org

Telephone (401) 737-6050

Notes

Notes

SENIOR DRIVING

SENIOR DRIVING ISSUES & CONCERNS

It is often difficult for aging individuals to recognize their changing abilities. Most seniors believe they will know when it is time to stop driving. For most people, driving is a sign of independence, control, competence and social responsibility. Consequently, giving up the keys can be devastating to seniors who view it as a loss of independence and self-sufficiency. The following article offers tips for seniors and others for recognizing unsafe driving, and guidance on handling decisions about driving.

First, it is important for seniors to know the signs of decreasing driving skills and adjust their driving habits to compensate for the decrease. For example, a senior who recognizes a decrease in driving skills could restrict his or her driving to:

- Daylight hours

- Off-peak traffic hours

- Familiar roads

- Shorter trips

- Lower speed roads

The AARP has published a "Close Call Quiz" as part of its Driver Safety Program to help drivers recognize diminishing driving skills. The AARP states that a "yes" answer to any of the ten questions may indicate that the driver perhaps had a close call for an accident. The ten questions are as follows:

1. Do you sometimes say, "Whew, that was close!"

2. At times, do cars seem to appear from nowhere?

3. At intersections, do cars sometimes proceed when you felt you had the right of way?

4. Are gaps in traffic harder to judge?

5.   Do others honk at you?

6.   After driving, do you feel physically exhausted?

7.   Do you think you are slower than you used to be in reacting to dangerous driving situations?

8.   Have you had an increased number of near accidents in the past year?

9.   Do you find it difficult to decide when to join traffic on a busy interstate highway?

10.   Do intersections bother you because there is so much to watch for in all directions?

Family, friends, physicians, care-managers and other individuals close to a senior are pivotal in identifying a senior's functional limitations that may impair driving performance and lead to unsafe decisions. Some physical signs that driving may be dangerous are loss of hearing, vision problems, health problems like arthritis, sleepiness, attention problems, and other medical conditions which may affect driving skills, such as dementia. Driving behavior that may indicate a person's driving threatens personal safety and that of others includes:

- Has difficulty following instructions

- Drifts into other lanes of traffic

- Stops abruptly without cause

- Presses simultaneously on the brake and accelerator while driving

- Delays changing lanes when an obstacle appears in the lane which he or she is driving.

- Does not use turn signals

- Straddles lanes

- Does not react to emergency situations

- Is increasingly nervous when driving

- Has difficulty seeing

Dealing with older family members diagnosed with dementia or Alzheimer's disease means family members need to take a more active role in making driving decisions. Since memory loss is associated with these diseases, the person often does not remember that he or she cannot drive. Explaining to the person can often lead to frustration and arguments. The Alzheimer's Association makes the following recommendations to family members:

- Begin with early planning. Have the person diagnosed with dementia sign an agreement with his/her family about driving. The Agreement can state who is allowed to make a decision to take away the keys, making that difficult decision that driving is no longer safe. Anyone can draft this simple Agreement for you and, while it may not be enforceable, it allows the senior to be an active participant in his/her future planning and decision making. Dignity cannot be overlooked.

- Get a prescription from the doctor that states "No driving".

- Have a physician order a driving evaluation. There is a list of driving evaluation resources in Rhode Island included in this section.

- Distract the family member who insists on driving, diverting his or her attention to something else.

- Control access to car keys by keeping them out of view, bending the keys, or filing them down. This should be a last resort.

- Disable the car by removing the distributor cap or unplugging the starter wire. This should be a last resort.

- Move the car out of sight.

- Sell the car and blame financial reasons for doing so, such as registration, insurance, gasoline, and regular maintenance costs.

Seek other sources of support, such as from your lawyer, geriatric care manager, and the Alzheimer's Association—RI Chapter. Most importantly, support from friends and family members is crucial to helping the senior through this time in his or her life.

Registry of Motor Vehicles-Operator Control Division

345 Harris Avenue

Providence, Rhode Island 02909

Phone: (401) 462-0802

Procedure: Anybody, including the physician, can send a letter to the Operator Control Division containing a short description of the driving concerns and incidents observed. The identity of the person who contacts the Division is kept confidential. When the letter is received, the driver of concern is asked to come into the office for a hearing. At the hearing, it is determined whether or not a road test or further evaluation is needed. After the evaluation, a decision will be made regarding the status of the driver's license, including possible suspension or revocation.

Cost: Free

NOTES AND NUMBERS

Rhode Island Department of Rehabilitative Medicine

Phone: (401) 444-5418

Contact: Laura Richard

Procedure: The driver of concern can be self-referred or can be referred by a physician. After an in-office clinical assessment is performed, there may be a road test. The report is prepared and given to the driver of concern and their family or friend. A report is also sent to the referring physician.

Cost: Insurance may pay for in-office clinical assessment. The on road evaluation is $150.

NOTES AND NUMBERS

Notes

Notes

TRANSPORTATION PROGRAMS

THE RIDE PROGRAM

Phone: (401) 461-9760

www.RIPTA.com

The RIde program provides transportation for individuals with disabilities and seniors. It is based on the eligibility requirements of several state agency programs.

The Division of Elderly Affairs, The Department of Human Services, Rhode Island Public Transit Authority, and a group of ARC's of Rhode Island are the major funding agency partners in the RIde Program. Some towns and nonprofit agencies also participate.

Each agency has its own program eligibility rules. RIde coordinates share ride services among all eligible passengers. Call for more detailed information or to schedule a reservation.

NOTES AND NUMBERS

RHODE ISLAND PUBLIC TRANSIT AUTHORITY (RIPTA)

265 Melrose Street

Providence, RI 02907

Phone: (401) 784-9500

www.RIPTA.com

Rhode Islanders of any age who have a disability may be eligible for Americans with Disabilities Act (ADA) Paratransit Services from the Rhode Island Public Transit Authority (RIPTA) curb-to-curb transportation service to people with disabilities which prevent them from using regular RIPTA bus service. This service is provided along existing RIPTA service corridors at a cost of twice the standard bus rate for all riders. To apply, call (401) 784-9500.

RIPTA bus passes cost residents aged 65 or older $5 and are valid for 5 years. Qualified riders who have a disability pay $2 for their 2-year pass. Pass holders pay half-fare on off-peak hours, weekends, and holidays. Bus pass holders enrolled in Medical Assistance (Medicaid) or RIPAE Level One income guidelines may apply for the No Fare program and ride free during all hours. Call RIPTA at 781-9400 for details and/or more information.

Notes

Notes

SENIOR IDENTIFICATION CARDS

SENIOR IDENTIFICATION CARDS

The Rhode Island Division of Motor Vehicles issues photo identification cards to Rhode Island residents age 59 and older and adults with disabilities. You must have proof of residence, proof of age, proof of signature, and proof of disability if under the age of 59. There is no fee.

The following Department of Motor Vehicle sites offer Senior Identification Cards:

Middletown DMV

73 Valley Road, Middletown, RI

Open Monday through Friday, 8:30am—3:30pm.

Pawtucket DMV

100 Main Street, Pawtucket, RI

Open Monday through Friday, 8:30am—3:15pm.

Wakefield

Stedman Government Center, Tower Hill Road, Wakefield, RI

Open Wednesday and Thursday, 8:30am-3:30pm.

Warren DMV

1 Joyce Street, Warren, RI

Open Tuesdays from 8:30am –3:30pm.

Woonsocket DMV

217 Pond Street, Department of Labor Bldg., Woonsocket, RI

Open: Tuesday through Friday, 8:30am –3:30pm.

MEAL ASSISTANCE PROGRAMS

THE OCEAN STATE SENIOR DINING PROGRAM:

The Ocean State Dining Program provides nutritionally balanced, hot lunches served five days a week at more than 75 meal sites for persons who are 60 years of age or older or disabled. In the case of a married couple, one person must be 60 years of age or older.

Seniors may donate to the cost of the meal, but no one is refused a meal if unable to contribute. Transportation to the nearest meal site is available. At least 24 hours notice is required for reservations. For information on meal site near you, please visit dea.ri.gov.

70 Bath Street

Providence, RI 02908

Phone: (401) 351-6700

www.rimeals.org

For over 40 years, Meals on Wheels of Rhode Island has provided home delivered and congregate meals to Rhode Island seniors. Providing necessary nutrition, the meals contribute to continuing independence for many seniors; keeping them in their homes rather than in an institutional setting. *There is no charge* for home delivered or congregate meals, however a $3.00 donation per meal is suggested.

The Meals on Wheels of Rhode Island Home Delivered Meal Program services almost 4,000 individuals annually. To be eligible to receive meals one must have an inability to cook due to a physical/ psychological impairment, live alone (with no help preparing meals), be 60 years of age or older (or on the DEA or DHS waiver program), have no help preparing meals, and be unable to drive or attend a congregate meal site.

For Providence area seniors who are able to leave their homes, the *Congregate Meal Program* provides a delicious hot meal in a community setting. Congregate meals keep seniors engaged in a social environment, while also offering nutritional workshops, newsletters, and more. There are three Providence locations and diners "pay" using a voucher.

For information on receiving meals, obtaining vouchers, or volunteering for Meals on Wheels programs, please call (401) 351-6700.

The Rhode Island Community Food Bank

200 Niantic Avenue

Providence, RI 02905

(401) 942-6325

www.rifoodbank.org

❃

The Rhode Island Coalition for the

Homeless

1070 Main Street

Pawtucket, RI 02860

(401) 721-5685

❃

Crossroads Rhode Island

160 Broad Street

Providence, RI 02909

(401) 521-2255

❃

Comprehensive Community Action Program

311 Doric Avenue

Cranston, RI 02921

(401) 467-9610

FOOD STAMP PROGRAM (SNAP)

www.dhs.ri.gov

The Supplemental Nutrition Assistance Program (SNAP) helps low-income households purchase food. Possible deductions from gross income may include a standard deduction for household and telephone expenses, an earned income deduction for working households and specified deductions for medical expenses and excess shelter costs. Adults who are eligible for the Food Stamp program receive their benefits using a special Electronic Benefit Transfer (EBT) card. Individuals can use their EBT card at grocery and retail food stores across the state. To apply for SNAP visit www.dhs.ri.gov.

Notes

PRESCRIPTION ASSISTANCE PROGRAMS

RIPAE

The Rhode Island Pharmaceutical Assistance to the Elderly (RIPAE) program pays a portion of the cost of Category A prescriptions used to treat the following:

- Alzheimer's disease
- Anti-infectives
- Arthritis
- Parkinson's disease
- Diabetes
- High blood pressure
- Heart Problems
- Cancer
- Depression
- Urinary inconsistence
- Circulatory insufficiency
- Chronic respiratory conditions
- High cholesterol
- Osteoporosis
- Asthma
- Glaucoma
- Mineral supplements
- Prescriptions vitamins

RIPAE also offer limited coverage for the cost of injectable prescription drugs used to treat Multiple Sclerosis.

RIPAE enrollees can purchase all other FDA-approved Category B prescriptions (except for those used to treat cosmetic conditions) at the RIPAE discounted price. Additionally, no state co-pay is needed for medications in this category.

Also under RIPAE, Rhode Island residents between 55 and 64 who are receiving Social Security Disability Income payments and who meet specified income limits, can purchase medications (except those prescribed for cosmetic conditions) at a discounted price.

For more specific questions regarding ones annual income and program eligibility please contact RIPAE at (401) 462-3000.

PHARMACEUTICAL RESEARCH AND MANUFACTURERS OF AMERICA

Many pharmaceutical manufacturers yield some of their drugs available free of charge to patients who have trouble paying for them. These voluntary programs, where each manufacturer creates its own eligibility criteria, typically require a physician to make direct contact with the selected manufacturer. Available drugs are generally used to treat long term illnesses.

For more information please contact the Pharmaceutical Research and Manufacturers of America at (202) 835-3400 or visit *www.phrma.org.*

UNIVERSITY OF RHODE ISLAND (URI) PHARMACY OUTREACH PROGRAM

This program assists Rhode Island residents regarding the availability of free or low cost medications through the Medication for the Needy Program. The program also provides educational seminars, health screens, and discussion groups on health related topics. Pharmacist are readily available to answer medication questions.

For more information please contact the University of Rhode Island (URI) Pharmacy Outreach Program at **(800) 215-9001** or visit *www.uri.edu/pharmacy/outreach.*

Notes

Notes

VETERANS SERVICES & RESOURCES

Middletown VA Community Based Outpatient Clinic One

Corporate Place

West Main & Northgate

Middletown, RI 02842

Phone: (401) 847-6239

Fax: (401) 847-8057

The Middletown VA facility provides comprehensive health care to veterans residing in Newport, Bristol, and Washington Counties. Every patient has a primary care provider who coordinates his or her health care needs. You can contact the Clinic for information on how to enroll or to arrange for a tour.

The Cremation Society of Rhode Island

571 W. Greenville Road, P.O. Box 216

North Scituate, RI 02857

Phone: (401) 647-0620

Toll Free: (800) 941-2211 (Available 24 Hours a Day)

www.csori.com

Under certain circumstances, the Veterans Administration provides cash benefits for reimbursement of burial expenses, a burial plot allowance, transportation allowance, a United States flag, Headstone or Marker, and free Grave Space.

The Providence Regional Office of the
Veterans Benefits Administration

380 Westminster Street

Providence, RI 02903

Phone: (800) 827-1000

www.va.gov

The Providence Regional Office is responsible for the management of most non-medial benefits provided by the Veterans Administration, including compensation, pension, vocational rehabilitation and counseling.

The Providence VA Medical Center

830 Chalkstone Boulevard

Providence, RI 02908

Toll Free: (866) 590-2976

Fax: (401) 457-3370

www.providence.va.gov/about

The Providence VA Medical Center provides outpatient and inpatient healthcare to veterans residing in Rhode Island and southeastern Massachusetts. A Primary Care Provider coordinates each patient's medical care, patient education needs and referrals to any of the medical centers 32 sub-specialty clinics. The Medical Center's Ambulatory Care Program is supported by a general medical, surgical, and psychiatric inpatient facility fully-accredited by the Joint Commission on the Accreditation of Healthcare Organizations (JCAHO). The medical center delivers a broad range of services in medicine, surgery, and behavioral sciences and is currently operating 73 beds.

The Rhode Island Veterans Affairs Office

480 Metacom Avenue

Bristol, RI 02809

Phone: (401) 253-8000 *695

Fax: (401)254-2320

www.dhs.state.ri.us

The Rhode Island Veterans Affairs Office offers Veterans benefit counseling including a the processing of all applications for admissions to the RI Veterans Home in Bristol, casework, counseling, referral and claims relating to pensions, compensations and Social Security. The Office also offers social services to Rhode Island armed forces personnel, veterans, and their dependents who are seeking assistance.

The Rhode Island Veterans Cemetery

301 South County Trail

Exeter, RI 02822

Phone: (401) 268-3088

www.dhs.state.ri.us

The Rhode Island Veterans Cemetery is comprised of 265 acres of land in Exeter, providing a final resting place for honorably discharged Rhode Island Veterans who have served during wartime, and their dependents. Eligibility requirements: the Veteran must have been discharged with "Honorable Service," have entered into the service from Rhode Island or have lived in Rhode Island two years prior to death, have had active duty during wartime, two or more consecutive years of active duty during peacetime, or have twenty years of National Guard Reserve time.

The Rhode Island Veterans Home

480 Metacom Avenue

Bristol, RI 02809

Phone: (401) 253-8000

The Rhode Island Veterans Home is a 110 Acre complex located on Mount Hope Bay. The mission of the Home is to provide quality nursing and residential care to eligible Rhode Island Veterans and their dependents and/or survivors to improve their physical, emotional, and economic well-being

The Home has 260 nursing care beds in three skilled and semi-skilled units and two ambulatory care units with an additional 79 beds.

Eligibility requirements: the Veteran must have been discharged with "Honorable Service" and have entered into the service from Rhode Island or have lived in Rhode Island two years prior to death. If eligible, a portion of the Veteran's income is applied and the need for Medicaid reduced.

Notes

VA CONTRACTED NURSING HOMES

The Veterans Administration contracted nursing homes receive benefits from the federally funded VA program. If eligible, the resident does not have any private payment to the nursing home. To be eligible, the resident must have a 70%-100% service related disability and be receiving a Veteran's Pension as a result of the service related disability. These eligibility rules differ from the state run Veterans Home.

The following are Rhode Island VA Contracted Nursing Homes:

Coventry Center, 10 Woodland Drive, Coventry, RI
Telephone (401) 826-2000

Hebert Health and Rehabilitation, 180 Log Road, Smithfield, RI
Telephone (401) 231-7016

Morgan Health Center, 80 Morgan Avenue, Johnston, RI
Telephone (401) 944-7800

Orchard View Manor,, 135 Tripps Lane, Riverside, RI
Telephone (401) 438-2250

Pine Grove Health Center, 999 South Main Street, Pascoag, RI
Telephone (401) 568-3091

Silver Creek Manor, 7 Creek Lane, Bristol, RI
Telephone (401) 253-3000

Trinity Health and Rehabilitation, 4 Saint Joseph Street,
Woonsocket, RI
Telephone (401) 765-5844

SENIOR ADVOCACY GROUPS & CONSUMER PROTECTION

CONSUMER PROTECTION

The Better Business Bureau

The Better Business Bureau tracks information on business in Rhode Island and other states. If you have a complaint against a business, or wish to inquire about a business prior to engaging services, call 1-800-422-2811 for more information, or visit www.rhodeisland.bbb.org.

National Do Not Call Registry

This Registry allows individuals to limit the number of phone call received by telemarketers. For more information, call 1-888-382-1222, or visit www.donotcall.gov.

Attorney General's Consumer Protection Unit

The Rhode Island Consumer Protection Unit handles complaints against Rhode Island businesses. If you feel as though you have been victimized by a scam, fraud, or scheme, you should call and you should also contact your local police department. For more information, call 401-274-4400.

LEGAL SERVICES

Rhode Island Disability Law Center www.ridlc.org

275 Westminster Street, Suite 401   Phone: 401) 831-3150

Providence, RI 02901   TTY (401) 831-5335

The Rhode Island Disability Law Center provides free legal assistance to disabled residents. Services include individual legal representation to protect rights or to secure benefits and services, self-help information, educational programs and administrative and legislative advocacy.

Rhode Island Legal Services Senior Citizens Program

56 Pine Street   Phone: (401) 274-2652

Providence, RI 02903   1-800-662-5034

TTY: 401-272-5335

The Rhode Island Legal Services Senior Citizens Program *helps low income persons age 60 and older* with legal advice and assistance for housing, Social Security, Medicaid, Medicare, and Food Stamp matters.

The Rhode Island Advisory Commission on Aging
(401) 462-0509

The commission was created in 1977 and advises the Governor and the Director of the Division of Elderly Affairs regarding issues and problems confronting elders and adults with disabilities.

❋

The Rhode Island Forum on Aging
(401) 462-0509

The Forum was established in 1991 and provides a focal point on aging issues, provides information on these issues, and establishes priorities for advocacy.

❋

The Rhode Island Long Term Care Coordinating Council
(401) 222-2371

The Council was created in 1987 and is committed to bringing quality, affordable and accessible long term care to Rhode Islanders.

❋

Senior Action in a Gay Environment
(401) 751-1487

SAGE offers support and social opportunities to elder gay persons.

❋

The Rhode Island Bar Association Legal Referral Service for the Elderly
(401) 521-5040

The Rhode Island Bar Association offers a reduced-fee program to moderate income seniors and a no-fee program for low income seniors.

The AARP

1-866-542-8170

10 Orms Street, Providence, RI 0296

AARP-Rhode Island is a non-profit, non-partisan organization for those 50 and older. AARP lobbies federal and state government for programs and services that enhance the quality of life for seniors.

www.aarp.org/ri

✳

The POINT

401-462-4444 or 401-462-0740 TTY

The POINT is Rhode Island's Aging and Disability Resource Center. They can provide information about available services and meet with you to discuss your options and the resources available to you.

The POINT is located at the United Way of Rhode Island

50 Valley Street

Providence, Rhode Island 02909

www.ThePointRI.org

✳

THE NATIONAL ACADEMY OF ELDER LAW ATTORNEYS

RHODE ISLAND CHAPTER

www.rinaela.com or www.naela.org

The NAELA membership is comprised of Rhode Island attorneys who deal with legal issues affecting people as they age and people with disabilities.

SENIOR AGENDA COALITION OF RHODE ISLAND

70 Bath Street

Providence, RI 02908

Phone: (401) 952-6527

www.SeniorAgendaRI.org

The Senior Agenda Coalition is a diverse coalition of activists and groups that advocate for the elderly organized to develop a common agenda to improve the quality of life of older Rhode Islanders. The coalition empowers people and organizations to discuss issues, promote legislation, and influence policies of both public and private institutions to further the common agenda.

One of the Coalition's greatest strengths is the ability to engage coalition members in their mission and work collaboratively with other organizations. Their intent and core purpose is to create and sustain this collaborative effort.

Campaigns include advocacy at the State House by seniors and advocates, attending all hearings on top priority bills, attending meetings with legislators at the Statehouse and in their districts, petitions, phone calls, and press events. Efforts are focused on monitoring the implementation of laws and working with the State Departments on regulation of programs.

In addition to the valuable research of our Best Practices Reports and Senior Agenda Fact book, they offer Elder Policy Advocate training which helps the Senior Agenda develop a base of trained advocates. These trainings educate seniors and advocates on how policy works, why it is important, and how to share stories.

The Senior Agenda Coalition also holds Senior Issues Candidates' Forums during election years. The Coalition has had great success sponsoring these highly attended events in the past. These forums help the Coalition build relationships with the candidates once they are in office, generate a lot of press, and help to educate and motivate seniors and advocates to push for legislation that benefits the elderly.

Notes

Notes

THE ALZHEIMER'S ASSOCIATION
RHODE ISLAND CHAPTER

ABOUT THE RHODE ISLAND CHAPTER
—A LETTER FROM THE EXECUTIVE DIRECTOR—
Donna M. McGowan

"The compassion to care, the leadership to conquer." That describes the work of the Alzheimer's Association.

The Rhode Island Chapter is a private, non-profit organization that provides education, personal support, and advocacy around key issues of concern to those persons in Rhode Island affected by this disease. It is supported solely through contributions from individuals as well as by public and private grants.

The services of the Rhode Island Chapter seek to assist both the 25,000 people in the State who have the disease and their care partners.

- The Early Stage Live and Learn Program utilizes a public library and other community sites to provide meaningful activities and socialization for those in the beginning stages of Alzheimer's disease.

- The agency HELPLINE provides 24 hour access to information and referral. (1-800-272-3900)

- Affiliated statewide support groups and community education presentations reach caregivers throughout Rhode Island.

- Medic Alert and Safe Return, the nationwide identification/registration system gives more peace of mind when families are faced with wandering of loved ones with Alzheimer's disease.

- A research lecture, every November, informs the statewide community of the status of progress in finding better treatment and ultimately, a cure.

All family services are free of charge.

The RI Chapter offers a wide variety of training geared to health care professionals. Staff at home care agencies, adult day centers, assisted living and nursing facilities learn how to manage the needs of Alzheimer patients. Special Care Units are examined by Chapter staff to provide greater assistance to those who care for people in later stages of the disease.

The Alzheimer's Association website helps both professionals and family members to gain extensive information on all aspects of Alzheimer's. A resource library in the RI Chapter office offers a plethora of valuable resources as well.

The Alzheimer's Association-RI Chapter advocates to improve the long term care health delivery system. As a member of the State Long Term Care Coordinating Council and the Senior Agenda Coalition, the agency works in conjunction with other advocates to bring about improvements.

There are very few people whose lives are not touched by Alzheimer's disease. Because of this wide-ranging impact, the Rhode Island Chapter can always use help. We encourage you to contact us!

Rhode Island Chapter

245 Waterman Street, Suite 306

Providence, RI 02906

(401) 421-0008 or (800) 272-3900

www.alz.org/ri

Here are a few ways you can assist the Alzheimer's Association—
Rhode Island Chapter.

- **Participate in the Memory Walk**

   Memory Walk is the nation's largest event to raise
   awareness and funds for Alzheimer's care, support and
   research. You can be a walker, sponsor a walker, start your
   own team or volunteer. For more information,
   go to www.alz.org/memorywalk

- **Volunteer** your experience/expertise for community
   presentations or help out in the RI Chapter office

- **Make a donation** in memory of a loved one or to honor
   someone affected by the disease.

- **Purchase Live & Learn Note cards** created by the partici-
   pation of the Live & Learn Program. Cards are $5.00 for four
   cards. Proceeds support the Live & Learn Program.

- **Purchase Beaded Bookmarks** created by the participants of
   the Live & Learn Program. Bookmarks are $5.00 and proceeds
   support the Live & Learn Program.

- **Purchase a Forget-Me-Not Flower Pin**

   These pins are made in Rhode Island for Rhode Islanders
   with Alzheimer's disease. The pins cost $20 each. All
   proceeds from pin sales will directly help Rhode Island
   families dealing with the challenges of Alzheimer's disease.

THANKS FOR YOUR SUPPORT!

Contact the Rhode Island Chapter for further information about how you
can help.

(401) 421-0008 or 1-800-272-3900

MEDICALERT® + SAFE RETURN®

Alzheimer's Association MedicAlert® + Safe Return® is a nationwide identification, support and enrollment program working at the community level. The specially designed service provides assistance whether a person becomes lost locally or far from home. Assistance is available 24 hours, every day, whenever a person is lost or found. The Alzheimer's Association is the trusted resource for information, education , referral, and support millions of people affected by the disease, their families and caregivers.

With a $49.95 enrollment in the Alzheimer's Association MedicAlert® + Safe Return® program, you will receive the following products:

1)   Engraved identification bracelet or necklace and iron-on clothing labels

2)   Caregiver checklist, key chain, label pin, refrigerator magnet, stickers and wallet cards.

3)   For an additional $25, you'll receive caregiver jewelry.
In   an emergency, it alerts others that you provide care for a person enrolled in Safe Return®.

If an enrollee is missing, the Alzheimer's Association MedicAlert® + Safe Return® program can fax the person's information and photograph to local law enforcement.

If an enrollee is found, a citizen or law official can call the number on the identification products and MedicAlert® + Safe Return® can access enrollee information and notify listed contacts.

For further information contact the Alzheimer's Association—

Rhode Island Chapter at (401) 421-0008 or visit www.medicalert.org/safereturn

You can enroll in MedicAlert® + Safe Return® in

one of the following ways:

<u>Send a completed enrollment form, photograph and payment to:</u>

Alzheimer's Association Medic Alert® + Safe Return®

2323 Colorado Avenue

Turlock, California 95382

OR

Alzheimer's Association—Rhode Island Chapter

245 Waterman Street, Suite 306, Providence, RI 02906

(401) 421-0008

Enroll by phone by calling toll-free **1-888-572-8566** (24 hours a day, every day) with complete credit card information.

Log onto *www.medicalert.org/safereturn* to **enroll online**.

**

COMFORT ZONE

Comfort Zone is a web-based service that works with a variety of location devices to monitor the whereabouts of an individual with Alzheimer's. It is a full service application with 24-hour support *that allows family members to check on a person with Alzheimer's, no matter where they are in the country.* Those enrolled will also be enrolled in the MedicAlert/Safe Return Program.

For more information or to enroll in Comfort Zone, visit www.alz.org/comfortzone or call 1-877-259-4850.

ELDER/ADULT POLICE ALERT REGISTRATION

Alzheimer's disease causes millions of Americans to lose their ability to recognize familiar places and faces. Many people cannot even remember their name or address. They may become disoriented and lost in their neighborhood or far from home.

It is common for a person with Alzheimer's disease to wander, many repeatedly, during the disease process. This behavior can be dangerous, even life threatening to individuals and stressful for caregivers. It is a known fact that elders and adults with Alzheimer's disease, other types of dementia, or medical conditions causing confusion may wander away from even the most caring of environments. Law-enforcement officials are keenly aware of the need to act swiftly to find these individuals and return them to safety.

As a result, the "Elder/Adult Police Alert Registration" form was the creation of Northwest Links, a collaboration of social service agencies in the Northwest corner of Rhode Island. In partnership with police departments in this area and the RI Chapter of the Alzheimer's Association, this group identified the information families could provide to their local police department to create a profile of persons at risk of wandering. Along with a recent photo, the information on this form is designed to save precious time in launching the search.

To acquire a registration form, contact:

The Alzheimer's Association— Rhode Island Chapter
(401) 421-0008

LUNCH AND LEARN
LUNCH AND LEARN

The Alzheimer's Association—Rhode Island Chapter offers two workshops that can be brought to the workplace during lunchtime for employers and employees. Caregivers are often stressed by their numerous responsibilities to family, work and caregiving and often have little spare time to attend informational meetings. These workshops were designed to enable caregivers to receive current up to date information to help them in their caregiving and hopefully reduce their level of stress.

The workshops are a free service of the Alzheimer's Association.

Workshop 1: Maintain Your Brain

Launched in 2004, Maintain Your Brain™ is a public awareness program directed to 77 million American baby boomers. The workshop is reaching out to change the way the nation thinks about brain health, memory, healthy aging and Alzheimer's disease. Learning ways to keep your brain healthier as you age might also reduce your risk of Alzheimer's disease or other forms of dementia.

Workshop 2: Workplace 101-Alzheimer's Disease

This presentation is targeted to individuals who wish to learn more about Alzheimer's disease. Using brain images, it illustrates the difference between Alzheimer's and normal aging and how Alzheimer's affects the brain. Other sections explain the warning signs, how to get a diagnosis, key services offered by the Alzheimer's Association and hopeful advances in research.

Other Community Based Educational Programs Available

To sign up for a workshop or to find out more, contact the Alzheimer's Association—Rhode Island Chapter at (401) 421-0008.

Talking to Alzheimer's

Simple Ways to Connect When You Visit with a Family Member or Friend

By Claudia J. Strauss

Losing My Mind

An Intimate Look at Life with Alzheimer's

By Thomas DeBaggio

Speaking Our Minds

Personal Reflections from Individuals with Alzheimer's

By Lisa Snyder, LCSW

What To Do When The Doctor Says It's Early-Stage Alzheimer's

All the Medical, Lifestyle, and Alternative Medicine Information You Need to Stay Healthy and Prevent Progression

By Todd E. Feinberg, M.D. and Winnie Yu

My Journey into Alzheimer's Disease

Helpful Insights for Family and Friends

A True Story

By Robert Davis

Notes

Notes

CHRONIC DISEASE RESOURCES

ARTHRITIS: The Arthritis Foundation

2348 Post Road, Suite 204

Warwick, RI 02886

Phone: (401) 739-3773

www.arthritis.org

Call for information and programs that are designed to help those with arthritis live active lives through exercise, self-help, and support

programs.

DIABETES: American Diabetes Association

Phone: (401) 351-0498

www.diabetes.org

DIABETES: The Diabetes Resource Center

21 Peace Street

Providence, RI 02907

Phone: (401) 456-4419

The Diabetes Resource Center at St. Joseph Hospital addresses the needs of high risk diabetes patients, including the uninsured, under-insured, and homeless.

They help with crisis intervention, medication, medical supplies, case manage-ments, and education.

DOWN SYNDROME: The Down Syndrome Society of RI

99 Bald Hill Road

Cranston, RI 02920

Phone: (401) 463-5751

www.dssri.org

MUSCULAR DYSTROPHY:
The Muscular Dystrophy Association

931 Jefferson Boulevard, #1005

Warwick, RI 02886

Phone: (401) 732-1910

www.mda.org

The Muscular Dystrophy Association provides financial assistance for wheelchairs, leg braces, and communication devices. It also runs an equipment loan program and transportation to and from its clinic.

PARKINSON DISEASE
Rhode Island Chapter of the American Parkinson Disease Association (APDA)

Phone: (401) 736-1046

www.riapda.org

The APDA serves the patients and caregivers of Rhode Island through the Information and Referral Center at Kent Hospital. They also offer sup-port groups, education, and socialization.

For information regarding Alzheimer's Disease and Multiple Sclerosis, please see the Chapters in this Guide dedicated to those Chronic Diseases.

The ALS Assocation Rhode Island Chapter

email: info@alsari.org
Telephone (401) 732-1609

Just what is ALS?

ALS was first found in 1869 by French neurologist Jean-Martin Charcot, but it wasn't until 1939 that Lou Gehrig brought national and international attention to the disease. Ending the career of one of the most beloved baseball players of all time, the disease is still most closely associated with his name. Amyotrophic lateral sclerosis (ALS) is a progressive neurodegenerative disease that affects nerve cells in the brain and the spinal cord. Motor neurons reach from the brain to the spinal cord and from the spinal cord to the muscles throughout the body. The progressive degeneration of the motor neurons in ALS eventually leads to their death. When the motor neurons die, the ability of the brain to initiate and control muscle movement is lost. With voluntary muscle action progressively affected, patients in the later stages of the disease may become totally paralyzed.

Our Chapter offers a full range of services at no charge to guide and assist you as you learn more about ALS. Here you will find pertinent information for patients, caregivers, family members, friends and healthcare workers. Our staff is here Monday through Thursday to answer any questions you may have. Please don't hesitate to call or e-mail us for more information. Our services include: home visits, consultations, equipment loans, handicapped transportation, respite care, educational symposium, support groups and multidisciplinary care at the Louise Wilcox ALS Clinic.

ABOUT THE RHODE ISLAND CHAPTER

**National
Multiple Sclerosis
Society**

The mission of the National Multiple Sclerosis (MS) Society is to end the devastating effects of Multiple Sclerosis. Founded in 1946, the National MS Society supports more research and serves more people with MS than any national voluntary MS organization in the world. Since its founding, over $280 million has been invested in research to find the cause, treatments and cure for MS. The National MS Society is also the only national voluntary MS organization that meets the standards of all major agencies that rate the fiscal responsibility of non-profit groups.

The National MS Society, RI Chapter, is one of 59 chapters across the United States that are helping advance the Society's mission: to end the devastating effects of MS. Founded in 1953, the Rhode Island Chapter is a non-profit organization and meets all the standards of the National Charities Information Bureau. The chapter provides services and programs to approximately 21,000 people affected by MS throughout Rhode Island.

Multiple Sclerosis is a chronic, often disabling disease of the central nervous system. Symptoms may be mild such as numbness in the limbs, or severe – paralysis or loss of vision. Most people with MS are diagnosed between the ages of 20 and 40 but the unpredictable physical and emotional effects can last a lifetime. The progress, severity and specific symptoms of MS in any one person cannot be predicted, but advances in research and treatment are giving hope to those affected by the disease.

Multiple sclerosis affects nearly a third of a million people in the US and a new case is diagnosed every hour. MS strikes more women than men. It is neither fatal, contagious nor inherited; the cause is not known yet. Today, exciting research and new treatments offer hope and improve the quality of life for people with the disease.

The Rhode Island Chapter fulfills their mission by helping keep families together despite the strain of dealing with chronic illness, helping people with MS get and keep jobs, providing accurate and up-to-date information about MS, giving free counseling, running self-help groups, advocating for people with disabilities, referring people to medical professionals with expertise in the disease, and in every way encouraging empowerment. For thousands of people with MS, these things mean the difference between living a full and active life and just existing.

The National Multiple Sclerosis Society is proud to be a source of information about Multiple Sclerosis. To contact the Rhode Island Chapter, please call (401) 738-8383 or toll free 1-800-FIGHT-MS.

**National
Multiple Sclerosis
Society**

Rhode Island Chapter

Phone: (401) 738-8383

www.NationalMSSociety.org / RIR

THE BOSTON HOME

2049 Dorchester Avenue

Boston, MA 02124

Phone: (617) 825-3905

www.TheBostonHome.org

In 1881, Miss Cordelia Harmon, a trained nurse, started The Boston Home for permanently disabled persons who could not be cared for in their homes nor accommodated in area hospitals. Since the inception, high standards of compassion and care have been sustained by generous donations of time and funds– and the vital commitment of wonderful staff and volunteers.

The mission of The Boston Home is to meet the long-term health care and related service needs of physically disabled adults in an environment that fosters self-determination. The Boston Home has a distinct niche in the nursing home industry as a progressive long-term facility for adult residents with physical disabilities. This non-profit community specializes in caring for adults, primarily age 40-60, with advanced Multiple Sclerosis and other progressive neurological diseases.

For The Boston Home residents, facing their disabilities is an ongoing challenge. They experience devastating changes such as loss of independence and control over their lives; poor self-esteem; and functional losses in mobility, coordination, cognition, vision, and speech. And because these changes can be variable, unpredictable, and progressive, The Boston Home residents never know what tomorrow may bring. Consequently, they are forced to confront these losses at many times during the course of their lives -- starting at diagnosis and again at each exacerbation -- as they require additional care. Many also suffer from fatigue and loss of short-term memory. Residents learn that adjusting to MS is an continuous process and a constant battle against stress, fear, anxiety, anger, and depression.

At The Boston Home, residents are encouraged to work toward improving their quality of life by engaging in activities geared toward their interests and gaining support from each other. Residents are empowered by the technologies offered in The Boston Home's computer center, and often use e-mail and video-conferencing to communicate with friends and family. Many residents belong to The Boston Home organizations that meet on a regular basis. These groups include the Writing Group, where they can creatively explore their emotions and writing talents in a non-threatening environment; the Men's Discussion Group for men to share their viewpoints and even have heated debates on topics of interest; and the Resident Council, where residents can provide feedback on certain aspects of their care at The Boston Home. In addition to structured groups and hobbies, recreational activities such as poker games and cocktail hours promote social interaction.

Despite the disruption of their family and career goals due to illness, most of The Boston Home residents continue to realign their goals and face the ongoing challenges with dignity. The Boston Home residents are a remarkable group of individuals who work together with their peers and The Boston Home staff to live their lives to the fullest in a community-oriented environment.

LIVING WITH MULTIPLE SCLEROSIS ("MS")
—THE VOICE OF PAMELA LUEBECK—

After suffering from problems with visual acuity and keeping her balance, Pamela Luebeck sought medical attention for an evaluation. Through process of elimination and within a year of Pamela's first onset of symptoms, she was diagnosed at the young age of nineteen with intermittent exacerbated Multiple Sclerosis.

Pamela was treated with short doses of steroids and was able to finish college. After graduation, she went to work caring for disabled children. She experienced recurring vision problems, which she kept under control for a good period of time with steroid use. However, due to an extended amount of time off for treatment, Pamela eventually lost her job.

Thereafter Pamela lived at home with her parents, David and Verna Luebeck, while she underwent further testing. Pamela's parents cared for her intently during this time.

Luckily, Pamela's MS went into remission and she was able to move to Connecticut, where she purchased her own home and worked at a children's home as a child care supervisor and service coordinator. There in Connecticut she resided for twenty years, experiencing few medical problems.

One day while driving she started to experience vision problems and after having to pull over, she was rushed to the hospital in an ambulance. Doctors prescribed her new medication and again withdrew her driving privileges.

Unable to withstand the strain of the disease, her marriage failed. With the divorce came much stress which further induced Pamela's poor health conditions. Her MS worsened catastrophically.

In 2007, Pamela was transferred from a nursing home in Connecticut, to Saint Elizabeth's Home in East Greenwich for rehabilitation. Having Pamela in Rhode Island made more sense, since this was where her support system was.

After several years of being bounced between assisted living, hospital care, and nursing homes, Pamela now resides at Riverview Healthcare Center and she has finally found a "home".

"I think it's hard for people outside of a nursing home environment to deal with people like me, living with multiple sclerosis. We're a piece of work!" Pamela jokes. Pamela says she is doing "okay" now. "I have good days and I have bad days," she tells me. "Sometimes, I feel tired and I just need to rest. Living with multiple sclerosis has been frustrating and highly emotional."

Finding the appropriate support for her psychological issues has always been difficult for Pamela. Not many doctors or counselors make house calls today; at least not on a regular basis.

"Pamela is in a sort of doughnut hole", explains her attorney, Laura Krohn. "She is too healthy (and very young) to be the right candidate at nursing home, yet she has difficulty with movement (hence the nature of MS) so her ability to continue residing at an assisted living residence is uncertain. I do think The Boston Home is a right fit for Pam, but she is still somewhat ambulatory, so she is not a candidate for there either."

"The toughest part of Pamela's case has nothing to do with her legal issues; it is the non-legal issues such as the emotional stress and frustration in coordinating the appropriate care that Pam and her parents deal with every day", Attorney Krohn explains.

There is no special housing program for individuals with MS, which is why Pamela rehabilitated in a nursing home among seniors. If Pamela were non-ambulatory (completely unable to move without the aid of a wheelchair), she would be a candidate for the Boston Home, which is a care facility specifically for those with the disease.

Understandably, Pamela seems to have lost much self-esteem and says it is hard to ask for help. Her social worker explains that the best way to help Pam is to listen and be supportive.

While there are things Pamela can no longer do, like driving, the thing she misses most is her friends. "I feel like I woke up from a coma and I never had a chance to make my own decisions." Although she understands that her parents want the best for her, Pamela has a hard time living co-dependently. She confesses that she sometimes feels like a five-year old child again.

When I asked Pamela what advice she might give to others who could relate to her story and life struggle, she responded that people should "stick with it, no matter what! Don't be afraid to ask for help." She admits that she often has trouble following her own advice.

Pamela knows she is very fortunate to have the unwavering support of her parents and for this she says she is forever grateful. Although she is scared about her uncertain future, Pamela's wish is to someday live independently again. She has faith that someday, she just might.

Pamela Luebeck, 2008

Notes

CAREGIVER SUPPORT GROUPS

ALWAYS CALL FIRST TO CONFIRM TIME AND DATE

For an updated list of support groups please visit the Alzheimer's Association RI Chapter at www.alz.org/ri

East Greenwich General Caregiver Support Group

Leaders: Laura M. Krohn, Esq. and Alice Phaneuf

159 Division Street (located in Atria Harborhill)

East Greenwich, RI 02818

Phone: (401) 398-8383

Every Thursday: 6:00-8:00pm

www.seniorguideri.com

*****

Hope Alzheimer's Center

25 Brayton Avenue

Cranston, RI 02920

Phone: (401) 946-9220

2nd Thursday: 200-3:30pm

www.HopeAlzheimersCenter.org

*Adult Day Care Provided
*****

RI Mood & Memory Clinic

1018 Waterman Avenue

East Providence, RI 02914

Phone: (401) 435-8950

4th Monday: 1:30pm

www.RIMMRI.com

*Adult Day Care Provided

<u>Dora C. Howard Adult Day</u>

<u>Center</u> 715 Putnam Pike

Greenville, RI 02828

Phone: (401) 949-3890

4th Wednesday: 1:00-3:00pm

www.DoraCHoward.com

<u>Beechwood House</u>

10 Beach Street

North Kingstown, RI 02852 Phone:

(401) 268-1591

2nd Tuesday: 1:00-2:30pm

<u>Salvatore Mancini Center</u>

2 Atlantic Boulevard

North Providence, RI 02911 Phone:

(401) 553-1031 *1095

1st Wednesday: 10:30-11:30am

<u>Leon Mathieu Senior Center</u>

420 Main Street

Pawtucket, RI 02860

Phone: (401) 722-3569 * 310

4th Wednesday: 5:30pm

St. Frances de Sales
North Kingstown, RI

Phone: (401) 421-0008

1st Wednesday: 5:30-7:00pm

Lincoln Senior Center
Lincoln, RI

Phone: (401) 723-3270

3rd Thursday: 10:30am

Newport Hospital
Newport, RI

Phone: (520) 275-8818

3rd Tuesday 6:00-7:30pm

Coventry Senior Center
Coventry, RI

Phone: (401) 439-1634

1st Tuesday: 6:30pm

South Kingstown Senior Center
South Kingstown, RI

Phone: (401) 783-0960

2nd Wednesday: 1:15-2:45pm

Portsmouth Senior Center

Portsmouth, RI 02871

Phone: (401) 846-0727

Every Tuesday: 9:30am

www.PortsmouthRI.com/SrCtr.htm

VNS of Newport & Bristol

1184 East Main Road

Portsmouth, RI 02871

Phone: (401) 682-2100

2nd Thursday: 6:30pm

www.VNSRI.com

Alzheimer's Association—Rhode Island

Chapter Office 245 Waterman St., Suite 306 Room

506 **Providence**, RI 02906

Phone: (401) 440-3886 or (401) 421-0008

1st Wednesday: 6:30-8:00pm

1st Thursday: 6:00-7:30pm

Baptist Church of Warren

Warren, RI

Phone: (401) 396-5200

4th Wednesday: 6:30pm

Gentiva Hospice Care

Warwick, RI

Phone: (401) 738-1492

3rd Tuesday: 10:00-11:30am

Barrington Senior Center

Barrington, RI

Phone: (401) 434-0891

1st Monday 1:00-2:00pm

Barrington Congregational Church

Barrington, RI

Phone: (401) 245-3288

2nd and 4th Tuesday 1:00-2:30pm

Middletown Senior Center

Middletwon, RI

Phone: (401) 848-4119

4th Tuesday 11:00am-12:00pm

Cavalry United Methodist Church
Middletown, RI
Phone (401) 848-4119
1st and 3rd Tuesday 10:00-11:00am

TIPS FOR CAREGIVERS

- Pay attention to your own health. Take leisure time for yourself. Acknowledge fatigue and take care of it.

- Utilize the resources available to assist you. Accept help when it is offered to you.

- Get support by attending support group meetings.

- Be realistic about what you can do. Don't be afraid to acknowledge that your loved one's needs may be beyond your ability.

- Be certain your loved one has executed the proper documents, giving you the authority to handle his/her financial and medical affairs.

- Have a contingency plan in place in the event that there is an emergency or a drastic change in health of your loved one or yourself.

WEECOPAUG, RHODE ISLAND
© GERI BOSCALIA CRITZ, *CLINICAL LABORATORY SCIENTIST, RI HOSPITAL*

"THE MOST SATISFYING THING IN LIFE
IS TO HAVE BEEN ABLE TO GIVE A LARGE PART
OF ONE'S SELF TO OTHERS."

Windsor Gallery Room at Highland Court

101 Highland Avenue

Providence, RI 02906

Phone: (401) 725-5962

2nd Wednesday: 7:00pm-9:00pm

❋

Bear Hill Village

156 Bear Hill Road

Cumberland, RI 02864

Phone: (401) 333-7972

3rd Wednesday: 7:00pm-9:00pm

❋

Dare to Dream

Immaculate Conception Church Parish

Center 237 Garden Hills Drive

Cranston, RI 02920

Phone: (401) 944-3949

1st & 3rd Tuesday: 10:00am-11:30am

Hopkinton Police Station

406 Woodville Road

Hopkinton, RI 02804

Phone: (401) 491-9270

Last Monday: 10:30am-12:00pm

✻

In Touch

(A telephone support group for people

at home or in a long-term care

facility) Phone: (401) 738-8383

3rd Monday: 11:00am-12:00pm

✻

Key Club

Greenwood Community Church

805 Main Avenue

Warwick, RI 02886

Phone: (401) 826-9988

1st Wednesday: 11:30am-1:30pm

✻

MS Outlook

Warwick Public Library

600 Sandy Lane

Warwick, RI 02889

Phone: (401) 886-5827

3rd Tuesday: 7:00pm-9:00pm

Notes

Notes

GOVERNMENT RESOURCE LISTINGS

RHODE ISLAND DIVISION OF ELDERLY AFFAIRS (DEA)

35 Howard Avenue

Benjamin Rush Building 55

Cranston, RI 02920

(401) 462-3000

www.dea.state.ri.us

The DEA Home and Community Care Programs: These programs provide eligible seniors with innovative options to help them remain in the community and avoid premature institutionalization. These options are designed to assist the functionally impaired senior meet a wide variety of medical, environmental, and social needs. Based on eligibility, these programs may provide home health aide services, adult day services, a personal emergency response system, Meals on Wheels, Senior Companion, minor home modifications or minor assistive devices. If appropriate, placement in an assisted living facility may be made. For most programs, a person must be 65 or older, a resident of Rhode Island, and be basically homebound (unable to leave home without considerable assistance). For some persons on Medicaid, services may be provided at no charge. Others may have to make a contribution towards services.

For more information, call **(401) 462-0570.**

Case Management: Case management programs assist older Rhode Islanders who wish to remain at home for as long as possible. To qualify, Rhode Island residents must be aged 60 or older (or Alzheimer's victims of any age), homebound, frail or disabled and unable to remain at home without supportive care. Through case management services, clients receive an assessment of their needs. A case manager develops a plan of care which includes options for community based services. The case manager will assist in securing needed services, monitor the care plan, and offer training and support for family caregivers. Clients with limited incomes and few cash resources may qualify for free or reduced-cost home care services. For more information on your nearest agency please see the Division of Elderly Affairs Co-Pay Program Section of this Guide.

Senior Citizen Identification (ID) Cards: DEA issues cards to Rhode Islanders aged 60 and older and adults with a disability. These photo-identification cards contain the owner's name, address, date of birth, and signature. They are valid as proof of identification for cashing checks and other banking transactions involving government funds under $750 at Rhode Island financial institutions. ID cards are valid for five years from the date of issue and are issued weekdays at the DEA office from 9am-3pm. Seniors must present proof of age, such as a driver's license, birth certificate, or a RIPTA bus pass. Persons with a disability must present a current Social Security disability or Veteran Administration disability award letter. Two forms of verification are required for a DEA identification card. TAdditional information about the identification card program is available by calling DEA at **(401) 462-4000.**

The Rhode Island Registry of Motor Vehicles offers **free** identification cards to seniors and adults with disabilities.

For information on both programs, please visit www.dea.ri.gov/programs/idcards.

RHODE ISLAND DEPARTMENT OF HEALTH AND HUMAN SERVICES

www.dhs.ri.gov

Rhode Island has a large number of elderly citizens, many of whom may require assistance at some point to maintain or enhance their quality of life. The Department of Human Services provides the following services to eligible elderly Rhode Islanders.

Medical Assistance Program: Medical Assistance is available for individuals over age 65 and disabled individuals who are medically and financially eligi-ble.

Long Term Care: Long Term Care services are available for adults over age 65 and disabled individuals who require home or community based services. Institutional care is available if care at home or in the community is not possible.

Food Stamps (SNAP): The Food Stamp Program provides supplemental food income for single or married individuals over age 60. Eligibility and the amount of the food stamp benefits depends on the size of your family, your income and other resources. Qualify-ing individuals get an ATM card that can be used to purchase food at most supermarkets.

Medicare Premium Payment Program: Rhode Islanders over age 65 who receive Medicare may qualify to have part or all of their deductible or co-payments for Medicare paid for by the state.

Title XX Homemaker Program: This program provides home-maker services and/or personal care assistance to individuals on Supplemental Security Income (SSI) who do not qualify for one of the Home and Community-Based Waiver programs.

SSI Assisted Living Program: This program provides enhanced Supplemental Security Income payments to Assisted Living Facilities for those individuals who require supervision in a residential setting.

Notes

PRIVATE SENIOR RESOURCES

Rhode Island Assisted Living Association (RIALA)

2224 Pawtucket Avenue

East Providence, RI 02914

Phone: (401) 435-8888

Fax: (401) 435-8881

www.RIALA.org

RI Association of Facilities & Services for the Aging

(RIAFSA) 225 Chapman Street, Box 7

Providence, RI 02906

Phone: (401) 490-7612

Fax: (401) 490-7614

www.RIAFSA.org

Rhode Island Partnership for Home Care (RIPHC)

334 East Avenue

Pawtucket, RI 02860

Phone: (401) 722– 9090

Fax: (401) 728-6509

www.RIPHC.org

Rhode Island Health Care Association (RIHCA)

57 Kilvert Street

Warwick, RI 02886

Phone: (401) 732-9333

www.RIHCA.com

Rhode Island Health Center Association (RIHCA)

235 Promenade Street, Suite 104

Providence, RI 02908

Phone: (401) 274-1771

Fax: (401) 274-1789

www.RIHCA.org

A Place for Mom

Phone: (877) 885-8583

A Place for Mom provides free comprehensive resources about senior housing and eldercare options to seniors and families in need.

A Place for Mom helps to provide options in the following areas:

- Independent and Assisted Living Communities
- Alzheimer's and Dementia Care
- Respite Care, Skilled Nursing Care, Home Care

Elizabeth Buffum Chace Center

Post Office Box 9476

Warwick, Rhode Island 02889

Business Phone: (401) 738-9700

Crisis Hotline: (401) 738-1700

Fax: (401) 738-1713

Advocacy, support and protection for victims of domestic violence.

AgeWell RI

Phone: (401) 223-2335

Or (866) 524-3935

Email: Agewellri.org; website: jsari.org

The Jewish Seniors Agency, Jewish Family Services, and the Jewish Community Center have collaborated to form AgeWell RI, a "virtual agency" that is now providing a single point of access to senior services.

Notes

FUNERAL PLANNING

PRE-ARRANGING AND PRE-PAYING FOR YOUR FUNERAL

There are many reasons to arrange and pay for your funeral in advance. Some clients want to provide comfort and peace of mind for family and friends. In a time of crisis, planning a funeral can be very stressful and emotional. Pre-paying also secures the price and cost of services against future increases.

Pre-paying for funeral services is also a very useful way to spend down assets to accelerate Medicaid eligibility for those who are receiving long-term care. This is because the purchase of a pre-paid funeral policy for the applicant or his/her spouse is a permitted transfer under the Rhode Island Medicaid rules. If purchasing a pre-paid funeral for this purpose, be sure that it is *irrevocable.*

The pre-paid funeral may include the cost of the casket, embalming services, cremation services, transportation to the cemetery, internment, and other related costs.

Many individuals have mixed feelings about planning for their funerals in advance. I can't blame them; I mean, who really wants to die, never mind plan for dying! Regardless of this fear, once it is done, every client feels a sense of relief that their family will have less stress, and security that their wishes will be carried out.

Of course, before signing and conveying any money on any contract, it is wise to have it reviewed by an attorney. And, like any smart consumer, look for the best service and product for your money.

Note: For questions and consumer information on prearranging a funeral, or other funeral and burial/cremation information, contact the Rhode Island Funeral Directors Association at (401) 885-3760 or visit www.rifda.org.

Smith Funeral & Memorial Services
8 Schoolhouse Road
Warren, Rhode Island 02885
Phone: (401) 245-4999
www.CelebrateWithSmith.com

✸

George C. Lima Funeral Home, Inc.
367 High Street
Bristol, Rhode Island 02809
Phone: (401) 253-9594

✸

Sansone Funeral Home, Inc.
192 Wood Street
Bristol, Rhode Island 02809
Phone: (401) 253-7110
www.SansoneFuneralHome.com

✸

Wilbur-Romano Funeral Home
615 Main Street
Warren, Rhode Island 02885
Phone: (401) 245-6818
www.WilburRomano.com

If you are interested in purchasing an extra
copy, please visit us at
www.seniorguideri.com
or call (401) 398-8383

Carpenter-Jenks Quaker Lane Chapel
659 East Greenwich Avenue
West Warwick, Rhode Island 02893 Phone:
(401) 826-1600
www.CarpenterJenks.com

※

Gorton Funeral Home
721 Washington Street
Coventry, Rhode Island 02816
Phone: (401) 821-7306
www.GortonFuneralHome.com

※

Frank Trainor & Sons Funeral Home
Inc 982 Warwick Avenue
Warwick, Rhode Island 02888
Phone: (401) 461-4843

※

Hill Funeral Home Inc
822 Main Street
East Greenwich, Rhode Island 02818
Phone: (401) 884-9222
www.HillFuneralHome.com

※

Iannotti Funeral Home
415 Washington Street
Coventry, Rhode Island 02816
Phone: (401) 821-1100

※

Peter J. Barrett Funeral Home
1328 Warwick Avenue
Warwick, Rhode Island 02888
Phone: (401) 463-9000

Potvin & Son Funeral Home Inc
45 Curson Street
West Warwick, Rhode Island 02893
Phone: (401) 821-6868

❋

Prata-Murphy Funeral Home
78 Providence Street
West Warwick, Rhode Island 02893
Phone: (401) 821-6760
www.MurphyFuneralHomes.org

❋

Henault Gallogly Funeral Home
5 Eddy Street
West Warwick, Rhode Island 02893
Phone: (401) 821-8484
www.GalloglyFuneralHome.com

❋

Russell J. Boyle & Son Funeral Home
142 Centerville Road
Warwick, Rhode Island 02886
Phone: (401) 732-8800
www.BoyleAndSonFuneralHome.com

❋

Thomas & Walter Quinn Funeral Home
Inc 2435 Warwick Avenue
Warwick, Rhode Island 02889
Phone: (401) 738-1977
www.TheQuinnFuneralHome.com

Fern Acres Funeral Home
72 Willow Avenue
Little Compton, Rhode Island 02837
Phone: (401) 635-4757

❈

Hambley Funeral Home
30 Red Cross Avenue
Newport, Rhode Island 02840
Phone: (401) 846-0698
www.MemorialFuneralHome.com

❈

Connors Funeral Home
55 West Main Road
Portsmouth, Rhode Island 02871
Phone: (401) 683-2511
www.MemorialFuneralHome.com

❈

Memorial Funeral Home
375 Broadway
Newport, Rhode Island 02840
Phone: (401) 846-0350
www.MemorialFuneralHome.com

❈

O'Neill-Hayes Funeral Home
465 Spring Street
Newport, Rhode Island 02840
Phone: (401) 846-0932
www.ONHFH.com

❈

Pocasset Memorial Funeral Home, Inc.
462 Main Road
Tiverton, Rhode Island 02878
Phone: (401) 625-5945
www.Almeida-Pocasset.com

A. Tarro & Sons Funeral Home
425 Broadway
Providence, Rhode Island 02909
Phone: (401) 421-7971

✼

Anderson-Winfield Funeral Home, Inc.
605 Putnam Pike
Greenville, Rhode Island 02828
Phone: (401) 949-0180

✼

B. Maceroni & Sons Funeral Home, Inc.
1381 Smith Street
North Providence, Rhode Island 02911
Phone: (401) 353-2400
www.Maceroni.com

✼

Barry Stapleton Holdredge Funeral Home,
Inc. 684 Park Avenue
Cranston, Rhode Island 02910
Phone: (401) 461-5050
www.CranstonFuneral.com

✼

Bell Funeral Home, Inc.
571 Broad Street
Providence, Rhode Island 02907
Phone: (401) 331-0200
www.BellFuneralHome.net

Boucher Funeral Home, Inc.
272 Sayles Avenue
Pascoag, Rhode Island 02859
Phone: (401) 568-5760

❋

Bright Funeral Home
290 Public Street
Providence, Rhode Island 02905
Phone: (401) 331-9411
www.Bright-FuneralHome.com

❋

Brown Funeral Homes, Inc.
1496 Victory Highway
Oakland, Rhode Island 02858 Phone:
(401) 568-5500

❋

Butterfield Home and Chapel 500
Pontiac Avenue
Cranston, Rhode Island 02910 Phone:
(401) 461-0151
www.TheButterfieldHome.com

❋

Charles Coelho Funeral Home, Inc.
151 Cross Street
Central Falls, Rhode Island 02863
Phone: (401) 724-9440
www.CoelhoFuneralHome.com

Corrigan-Brown Funeral Home, Inc.

1496 Victory Highway
Oakland, Rhode Island 02858
Phone: (401) 568-5500

❋

Costigan-O'Neill Funeral Home, Inc.

220 Cottage Street
Pawtucket, Rhode Island 02860
Phone: (401) 723-4035
www.RIFunerals.com

❋

Curtis J. Holt's & Sons

510 South Main Street
Woonsocket, Rhode Island 02895
Phone: (401) 769-0133

❋

D. W. Bellows & Son

85 Park Place
Pawtucket, Rhode Island 02860
Phone: (401) 723-0084

www.BellowsFH.com

❋

Darlington Mortuary Of L Heroux & Son, Inc.

1042 Newport Avenue
Pawtucket, Rhode Island 02861
Phone: (401) 722-4376

S. DiPardo Memorial Chapel
Funeral Home

1583 Diamond Hill Road
Woonsocket, Rhode Island 02895
Phone: (401) 762-3746

❋

Robbins Funeral Home, Inc.
2251 Mineral Spring Avenue
North Providence, Rhode Island 02911
Phone: (401) 231-9307
www.RobbinsFuneralHome.com

❋

Olson & Parent Funeral Home
417 Plainfield Street
Providence, Rhode Island 02909
Phone: (401) 944-6460
www.OlsonParent.com

❋

Fournier & Fournier, Inc.
463 South Main Street
Woonsocket, Rhode Island 02895
Phone: (401) 769-0940

❋

Fournier & Fournier, Inc.
99 Cumberland Street
Woonsocket, Rhode Island 02895
Phone: (401) 769-0940

❋

Hoey-Arpin-Williams-King Funeral Home
168 Academy Avenue
Providence, Rhode Island 02908
Phone: (401) 272-6363
www.RIFuneral.com

J. J. Duffy Funeral Home, Inc.
757 Mendon Road
Cumberland, Rhode Island 02864
Phone: (401) 334-2300
www.JJDuffyFuneralHome.com

❋

James J. Gallogly & Sons Funeral Home, Inc. 671 Broad Street
Providence, Rhode Island 02907
Phone: (401) 331-7608
www.GalloglyFuneralHome.com

❋

Jones-Walton-Sheridan Funeral Home
1895 Broad Street
Cranston, Rhode Island 02905
Phone: (401) 781-1188
www.JWSFH.com

❋

Lachapelle Funeral Home, Inc.
643 Main Street
Pawtucket, Rhode Island 02860
Phone: (401) 724-2226

Lincoln Funer al Home, Inc.
1501 Lonsdale Avenue
Lincoln, Rhode Island 02865
Phone: (401) 726-4117

❋

Manning-Heffern Funeral Home
68 Broadway
Pawtucket, Rhode Island 02860
Phone: (401) 723-1312
www.ManningHeffern.com

❋

Max Sugarman Memorial Chapel
458 Hope Street
Providence, Rhode Island 02906
Phone: (401) 331-8094

❋

Marino Pontarelli Funeral Home
971 Branch Avenue
Providence, Rhode Island 02904
Phone: (401) 331-7390

❋

McAloon & Kelly Funeral Home
643 Main Street
Pawtucket, Rhode Island 02860
Phone: (401) 722-1527

❋

Menard's Funeral Home
127 Carrington Avenue
Woonsocket, Rhode Island 02895
Phone: (401) 762-1825

Merrick R. Williams Funeral Home
530 Smithfield Avenue
Pawtucket, Rhode Island 02860
Phone: (401) 723-2042
www.MerrickRWilliamsFH.com

✸

Monahan, Kelly, Drabble & Sherman Funeral
Home 230 Waterman Street
Providence, Rhode Island 02906
Phone: (401) 331-4592
www.MKDS.com

✸

Nardolillo Funeral Home, Inc.
1278 Park Avenue
Cranston, Rhode Island 02910
Phone: (401) 942-1220
www.NardolilloFH.com

✸

Pennine Funeral Home, Inc.
28 Grove Street
Providence, Rhode Island 02909
Phone: (401) 421-7739
www.PennineFuneralHome.com

✸

Perry-McStay Funeral Home, Inc.
2555 Pawtucket Avenue
East Providence, Rhode Island 02914
Phone: (401) 434-3885

Rebello Funeral Home, Inc.
901 Broadway
East Providence, Rhode Island 02914
Phone: (401) 434-7744
www.RebelloFuneralHome.com

※

Robbins Funeral Home
2251 Mineral Spring Avenue
Providence, Rhode Island 02911
Phone: (401) 231-9307
www.RobbinsFuneralHome.com

※

Romano & Sons Funeral Home
627 Union Avenue
Providence, Rhode Island 02909
Phone: (401) 944-5151

※

Romenski & Son, Inc.
342 High Street
Central Falls, Rhode Island 02863
Phone: (401) 722-7250

※

Russell J. Boyle & Son Funeral Homes
331 Smith Street
Providence, Rhode Island 02908
Phone: (401) 272-3100
www.BoyleAndSonFuneralHome.com

Sinai Mount Memorial Chapel

825 Hope Street
Providence, Rhode Island 02906

Phone: (401) 331-3337
www.DignityMemorial.com

❋

Skeffington Funeral Home

925 Chalkstone Avenue
Providence, Rhode Island 02908

Phone: (401)331-3900
www.SkeffingtonFuneralHome.com

❋

Smith-Mason Funeral Home, Inc.

398 Willett Avenue
East Providence, Rhode Island 02915

Phone: (401) 433-2300

❋

Tucker-Quinn Funeral Home, Inc.

649 Putnam Pike
Greenville, Rhode Island 02828

Phone: (401) 949-1370
www.TuckerquinFuneralHome.com

❋

William W. Tripp Funeral Home 1008

Newport Avenue
Pawtucket, Rhode Island 02861
Phone: (401) 722-2140
www.TrippFuneralHome.com

Winfield & Sons Funeral Home & Crematory, Inc.
Route 116
Scituate, Rhode Island 02857
Phone: (401) 647-5421
www.WinfieldAndSons.com

❋

Woodlawn Funeral Home
600 Pontiac Avenue
Cranston, Rhode Island 02910
Phone: (401) 421-0289
www.WoodlawnGattone.com

❋

W. Raymond Watson Funeral Home
350 Willett Avenue
Riverside, Rhode Island 02915
Phone: (401) 433-4400
www.WRWatsonFuneralHome.com

BLOCK ISLAND, RHODE ISLAND
© GERI BOSCALIA CRITZ, *CLINICAL LABORATORY SCIENTIST, RI HOSPITAL*

Avery Storti Funeral Service
88 Columbia Street
Wakefield, Rhode Island 02879
Phone: (401) 783-7271

❅

Buckler-Johnston Funeral Home
121 Main Street
Westerly, Rhode Island 02891
Phone: (401) 596-2465

❅

**Cranstons Of Wickford Funeral Home,
Inc.** 140 West Main Street
North Kingstown, Rhode Island 02852 Phone:
(401) 294-4013

❅

Forbes Funeral Home Inc
28 Columbia Street
Wakefield, Rhode Island 02879
Phone: (401) 789-6550

❅

Gaffney-Dolan Funeral Home Inc
59 Spruce Street
Westerly, Rhode Island 02891
Phone: (401) 596-2648

❅

Lawrence E. Jr. Fagan Funeral Home
825 Boston Neck Road
North Kingstown, Rhode Island 02852 Phone:
(401) 295-5603
www.TheQuinnFuneralHome.com

Nardollilo Funeral Home
1111 Boston Neck Road
Narragansett, RI 02882
Phone: (401) 789-6300
www.NardolilloFH.com

✳

Rushlow-Iacoi Funeral Home
64 Friendship Street
Westerly, Rhode Island 02891
Phone: (401) 596-2352
www.RushlowIacoiFuneralHome.com

✳

S. R. Avery Funeral Home
2A Bank Street
Hope Valley, Rhode Island 02832
Phone: (401) 539-2271

If you are interested in purchasing an extra
copy, please visit us at
www.seniorguideri.com

Notes

GLOSSARY

Adult Day Care

Adult day care is a planned program of activities designed to promote well-being though social and health related services. Adult day care centers operate during daytime hours in a safe, supportive environment. Nutritious meals that accommodate special diets are typically included, along with an afternoon snack.

Adult day care centers can be public or private, non-profit or for-profit. The intent of an adult day center is primarily two-fold:

- To provide older adults an opportunity to get out of the house and receive both mental and social stimulation

- To give caregivers a much-needed break in which to attend to personal needs, or simply rest and relax

Good candidates for adult day care are individuals who can benefit from the friendship and functional assistance a day care center offers or that may be physically or cognitively challenged but do not require 24-hour supervision.

Adult day dare center participants need to be mobile, with the possible assistance of a cane, walker or wheelchair, and in most cases, they must also be continent.

Common recreational activities include arts and crafts, musical entertainment, mental stimulation games, exercise, discussion groups, holiday and birthday celebrations, local outings, and intergenerational programs.

Besides recreational activities, some adult day care centers provide transportation to and from the center, social services including counseling and support groups for caregivers, and health support services such as blood pressure monitoring and vision screening. Often, Adult Day Care Centers provide health assessments and therapy if staffed with an RN and other health professionals. Other types of day care provide social and health services specifically for individuals with Alzheimer's (including earl-onset) or a related type of dementia.

The cost for an adult day care center ranges but is typically set on a per-day basis. Many facilities offer services on a sliding fee scale, meaning that what you pay is based on your income and ability to pay. Be sure to ask about financial assistance.

Payment options will depend on the individual's situation, and may include private-pay, long-term care insurance, Medicare and Medicaid.

Assisted Living

An assisted living residence provides care for seniors who need some help with activities of daily living yet wish to remain as independent as possible. Essentially, assisted living is the middle ground between independent living and nursing homes. The goal of assisted living is to provide seniors with an environment that encourages as much autonomy as they are capable of, while providing socialization, safety, and family peace of mind. Most residences offer 24-hour supervision and an array of support services, with more privacy, space, and dignity than many nursing homes, and at a lower cost.

Assisted Living Residences are also called personal care homes, residential care facilities, domiciliary care, sheltered housing, and community residences.

An Assisted Living Residence helps seniors with personal care/ custodial care, such as bathing, dressing, toileting, eating, grooming and transport.

Daily contact with supervisory staff is the defining characteristic of an Assisted Living Residence. Medical care is usually limited in an Assisted Living Residence, but it is possible to contract for other medical needs.

Assisted Living Residences are owned and operated by both for-profit and non-profit organizations and can range in cost depending on where you live. Fees may be inclusive or there may be additional charges for special services.

Costs are generally lower than for full-time home health services or nursing home care. Payment options will depend on the individuals situation, and may include private-pay, long-term care insurance, and Medicaid.

Geriatric Assessment

A geriatric assessment is a comprehensive evaluation designed to optimize an older person's ability to enjoy good health, improve their overall quality of life, reduce the need for hospitalization and/or institutionalization, and enable them to live independently for as long as possible.

Typically, the assessment is done by a team of experts which often include geriatricians, neurologists, social workers, therapists, dieticians, psychologists, pharmacists, and geriatric nurse practitioners.

Geriatric Care Manager

A geriatric care manager (GCM) is a professional with specialized knowledge and expertise in senior care issues. Ideally, a GCM holds an advanced degree in gerontology, social work, psychology, nursing, or a related health and human services field.

Sometimes called case managers, elder care managers, service coordinators or care coordinators, GCMs are individuals who evaluate your situation, identify solutions, and work with you to design a plan for maximizing your elder's independence and well being.

Geriatric care management usually involves an in-depth assessment, developing a care plan, arranging for services, and following up or monitoring care. While you are not obligated to implement any part of the suggested care plan, geriatric care managers often suggest potential alternatives you might not have considered, due to their experience and familiarity with community resources. They can also make sure your loved one receives the best possible care and any benefits to which they are entitled.

Geriatric Neurologist

As a Geriatric subspecialty, Geriatric Neurology focuses on neurological diseases and disorders that are common to older adults. The correct diagnosis of neurological disorders in older adults is difficult because signs of disease may mimic normal signs of aging. In addition, patients frequently have more than one neurological problem at a time. This subspecialty the result of growing recognition that neurological conditions may present differently in middle or late life, and that the older adult may require different treatments than younger patients.

One of the most common geriatric neurology problems is memory loss and dementia. In addition, many other neurological disorders are more common with age including, stroke, Parkinson's disease, seizures, and gait disorders. The subspecialty of geriatric neurology focuses on evaluating and treating these common neurological conditions in older adults.

Geriatric Physician

A Geriatrician is a medical doctor who specializes in the medical needs of seniors. All seniors should consult with a geriatrician, even if they already have a family physician.

Home Health Care

Home care typically refers to medical and/or non-medical services that assist individuals with daily living.

Home care is becoming an increasingly popular choice for care because it enables individuals to remain in their own environments longer and helps families better plan for the care of a loved one.

Many families utilize home care agencies to supplement the services they cannot perform themselves for a loved one due to work and other family commitments. These agencies provide an extra pair of hands and assist in the overall care management of a loved one.

Most agencies can provide services for as little as six hours a week up to 24 hours a day, seven days a week. The schedules are usually determined during the assessment process and vary depending on the needs of both the family caregiver and the needs of the client.

Caregivers need to be reminded that they are at health risk if they try to take on too much and forget to take care of themselves. *It is just as important that the caregiver is getting proper nutrition, rest, and exercise as it is for the person they are caring for.*

Hospice

Hospice represents a compassionate approach to end-of-life care. Hospice care is an option for people whose life expectancy is approaching six months or less. Hospice programs focus on all the aspects of life and well-being including the physical, social, emotional, and spiritual realms. There is no age restriction for hospice care and anyone in the last stages of life is eligible for the services. While some hospitals, nursing homes and other health care facilities provide hospice care onsite, hospice most often takes place in the comfort of your own home, allowing you to remain in familiar surroundings as you prepare for a meaningful life conclusion.

Hospice services are generally structured according to a person's specific needs which often change over time. A hospice team may include any combination of the following services: Nursing Care, Social Services, Physician Services, Spiritual Support and Counseling, Clergy and other spiritual services, Home Health Aides and Homemaker Services, Trained Volunteer Support, Physical, Occupational, and Speech, Respite Care, Inpatient Care, and Bereavement Support.

Independent Living

Independent Living provides the greatest versatility and freedom. Independent Living for seniors refers to residence in a compact, easy-to-maintain, private apartment or house within a community of other seniors. The housing arrangement is designed exclusively for seniors, generally those aged 55 and older.

Independent Living for seniors is also known as Retirement Communities, Retirement Homes, Senior Apartments, Senior Housing, and Independent Living Communities.

As the name implies, Independent Living is just that: the ability to maintain one's residence and lifestyle without custodial or medical assistance. If custodial or medical care becomes necessary, residents in Independent Living for seniors are permitted to bring in outside services of their choice. Some facilities even have a social worker on staff to assist in contacting agencies that provide medical or personal care. Many also are gated communities with their own security guards. Some senior apartment complexes provide community services such as recreational programs, transportation services, and meals in a communal dining room.

Medicaid

Medicaid is a federal-state partnership program which pays for about half of all long-term care costs in America. Medicaid eligibility is crucial for seniors who face the possibility of long-term nursing care.

Unlike Medicare, Medicaid is not an entitlement and eligibility is based on need (both medical and financial). The regulations that govern Medicaid eligibility are very complex and individuals should seek advice to navigate the rules and requirements properly.

Medicare

Medicare is a federal health insurance program for the elderly and the disabled. Medicare benefits are tied to Social Security benefits. The Medicare program consists of three parts: Medicare Part A which provides hospital insurance and skilled nursing insurance, Medicare Part B which provides medical insurance, and Medicare Part D which provides some coverage for prescription drugs. Unlike Medicaid, Medicare is an entitlement and is not based on financial need.

Respite Care

Respite care provides time off for family members or other caregivers who care for someone who is ill, injured or frail. It can take place in an adult day center, in the home of the person being cared for, or even in a residential setting such as an assisted living residence or nursing home.

Although there are different approaches to respite care, all have the same basic objective: to provide caregivers with planned temporary, intermittent, substitute care, allowing for relief from the daily responsibilities of caring for the care recipient. Respite care is essential for all caregivers in order to relieve stress and prevent burnout. For more information refer to the caregiver stress article in the support group section.

Senior Centers

Senior Centers are meeting places that are dedicated to helping seniors live meaningful lives of dignity, enjoyment and useful purpose. The centers' main focus is improving and enriching lives of seniors through programs, resources and volunteer work. They provide programs and services that enhance their social, physical and mental well-being.

Each town typically has its own Senior Center for the surrounding community. Membership fees vary for town and non-town members but prices are generally minimal. Most centers provide their own transportation.

Nursing Homes & Rehabilitation

A Nursing Home can provide custodial care and/or skilled nursing to provide 24 hour care to people who can no longer care for themselves due to physical, emotional, or mental conditions. A licensed physician supervises each patient's care and a nurse or other medical professional is almost always on the premises.

Skilled medical care includes services of trained professionals that are needed for a limited period of time following an injury or illness. This may include would care, I.V. administration and monitoring, physical therapy, speech therapy, occupational therapy, or administering and monitoring I.V. antibiotics for a severe infection. Skilled care may also be needed on a long term basis if a resident requires injections, ventilation or other similar treatment.

Custodial or personal care includes assistance with bathing, dressing, eating, grooming, transport, and incontinence care. This type of care may be a temporary or long-term need depending on the situation.

Nursing Homes and rehabilitation centers offer an array of services, in addition to the basic skilled nursing care and the custodial care. They provide a room (private or semi-private), all meals, some social activities, personal care, 24-hour nursing supervision and access to medical services when needed. In addition, many Nursing Homes provide respite care so that caregivers can have a break and interim medical care which is care after a hospital stay.

Support Group

A support group generally refers to a group of individuals who meet on a regular basis to exchange mutual support. They often focus on a shared area of difficulty, most often a disease or condition. Groups are organized at various locations but typically are facilitated by a social worker. Support groups are a crucial resource for caregivers because often the caregiver forgets to take care of him or herself while providing care and support to a loved one. In a support group environment, the caregiver can receive valuable support, advice, and resource information from other individuals familiar with the issues the caregiver is facing.